Old Fences,
New Neighbors

Peter R. Decker

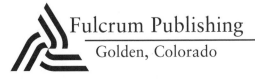

Fulcrum Publishing
Golden, Colorado

Library of Congress Cataloging-in-Publication Data

Decker, Peter R., 1934-
  Old fences, new neighbors / Peter R. Decker.
      p. cm.
  Originally published: Tuscon : University of Arizona Press, c1998. With new foreword.
  ISBN 1-55591-569-8 (pbk.)
  1. Ouray County (Colo.)--History. 2. Ouray County (Colo.)--Social conditions. I. Title.
  F782.O9D43 2006
  978.8'22--dc22

                                2005032460

ISBN-13: 978-1-55591-569-8
ISBN-10: 1-55591-569-8

Originally published in hardcover and paperback by the University of Arizona Press in 1998.

Printed in the United States of America

0 9 8 7 6 5 4 3 2 1

Design: Jack Lenzo
Cover image: Copyright © Eileen Benjamin
Map: Copyright © Full View Mapping, LLC.

Fulcrum Publishing
16100 Table Mountain Parkway, Suite 300
Golden, CO 80403
(800) 992-2908 • (303) 277-1623
www. fulcrumbooks.com

To Deedee

The ... rocky West is intruding a new and continental element into the national mind, and we shall have an American genius [ethos]. ... We must regard the **land** as a commanding and increasing power on the citizen, ... which promises to disclose new virtues for ages to come.

—Ralph Waldo Emerson, "The Young Americans"

Contents

In 1974, after a long birding trip across the country, I drove north from
Arizona over Red Mountain Pass and into Ouray. Though I'd grown
up in Colorado, I'd never been to Ouray County, isolated as it was, but
I was so mesmerized by the peaks and valleys, by the sheer beauty of
the place, that my first stop was at a real estate office. My wife and I
bought what was left of an original homestead that had been whittled
down to seventeen acres, part of it irrigated, at the foot of Log Hill
Mesa. In the ancient barn, two hundred yards from the house, I built
myself a writing room using hand tools and a Coors bottle for a level.
There was no electricity. I put in a floor, a woodstove, and several windows. I wrote short stories there on a standard typewriter and watched
the weather, the coyotes and weasels, the deer, the eagles. Birds were
numerous in migration—warblers, thrashers, hawks, cranes. The world
was right out any window.

   The task of the writer is to create an experience meaningful to
the reader, and landscape for me is always the beginning. My property
looked over vacant land—sage and rabbitbrush, sloping hillsides, Pinna-
cle Ridge to the east, Mount Sneffels to the south. It was at the very
end of the ditch, and the previous owner kept first-priority water rights.
In spring, with the snowmelt, there were no problems, but in summer
when the rainless clouds drifted off over Log Hill, getting water to my

hay meadow was an effort. I spent at least two hours every day walking up the ditch (there was a flume that carried water thirty feet above and over Dallas Creek) and cutting back the users who were taking my water. The experience led to a story, "Ditch Rider," in which the protagonist, Jack Lindstrom, is concerned about his son, who, earlier in the evening, before a date, had gone up to check water. Landscape: "That had been at six-thirty and still light. I hadn't noticed whether there was water until after dinner when I went out to take a piss and settle the calves. It was dark then, and the wind had stopped. A few thin clouds rolled above the dry pinyon mesa to the west. Chimney Peak and Courthouse, two granite blocks to the east, were slick with moonlight, and it was so bright I didn't need a flashlight. The ditch was empty. You could hear it was empty. But there had been water earlier because a sheen of mud-reflected moonlight, and water stood in the low spots."

I loved the place by being part of it: my property, the mesas and mountains, the sky. In my fiction, there are a dozen or more stories and a novel that use Ouray County as a backdrop, and I look back with fondness of experience and sadness at the changes that Peter Decker describes in *Old Fences, New Neighbors*. The country is in my body, as well as in my mind. Log Hill Mesa now has houses along its perimeter, and the vacant land beside my property (now sold) is filled with big houses, but I can still conjure up eagles that used to nest on the face of the cliff and the snow coming across the Dallas Divide. I still imagine running the Blue Lakes Trail, the Horsethief and Bear Creek Trails, the county roads. I smell elk. This landscape is home, even when I am not there.

I have ranched the same territory of the imagination as Peter Decker writes about, though he's a social scientist and I'm a storyteller. We're not that different. We have loved the same place by being a part of it, by living there. Through accident, I was for several years the city judge of Ouray and Ridgway, which made me friends and enemies both. I gave a man a small fine for speeding because he said he was taking his mother-in-law to the airport; and a motorcycle speeder came to my house six weeks in a row with twenty five dollars, and we talked books. Once I got in trouble with the Ridgway City Council for throwing out an ordinance that allowed a cow or a horse on an acre of land, but not a goat. The city was harassing the goat owners. These are still stories to be written.

But it's a bigger story. *Old Fences, New Neighbors* chronicles with precision and wit what has happened across the West in the last thirty years—the disruption and breakdown of the old ranching society and the order of human relationships based on work, and its replacement by a monied aristocracy that dominates with sheer economic resilience and without the necessity of connecting work to the land. "The Old West doesn't have much regard for the New West," Decker writes. "When local ranchers look at a hobby ranch ... purchased from money earned elsewhere, they are reminded that it is now impossible for their sons and daughters to buy a place of their own." Decker's clear style and wit is touched with sadness for the vanishing natives—not only of the Mountain Utes of Ouray County, but as well for the ranchers and land-lovers who are forced by capitalism to change their lives. The writer, however, cannot lament. He can only set down the truth as he sees it and hope that readers will understand and work in numbers toward a system of government and society that values the working man.

The truth is America's beautiful places—and Ouray County is among the most beautiful—belongs to the wealthy. The not-so-well-off are pushed to the edges of the landscape they first settled, or they move to cheaper but less beautiful places. For them, the beautiful places the world over are running out, as indeed they are for all of us.

—Kent Nelson
Author, *Land That Moves, Land That Stands Still*,
and winner of the Colorado Book Award for fiction

In the six years since the first appearance of this book, the biggest issue confronting residents of Ouray County and the town of Ridgway has been how to respond to the pressures of unabated growth.

In this ranching county, residents will soon outnumber the county's livestock population. New mailboxes at the hardware store are back-ordered. Ranchers continue to receive what they consider "outrageously high" offers for their land, especially if it is in sight of the mountains. Some ranchers are tempted to sell out; most are not. Realtors report that they are seeing a diaspora of urban dwellers seeking a safe, clean second-home setting in a small rural community that could be converted into a permanent home site in an emergency. To make room for new homes, ranchland continues to be subdivided, and the smaller ranches are absorbed into larger units of production. The newcomers arrive with their horse trailers and computers, ready to take up a new, "rural" lifestyle evoked, perhaps, from the pages of glossy magazines. City migrants from both coasts seek the psychic comfort of a small community and gradually work themselves into the organizations that glue a community together.

The sheer number of new residents has changed the county's character. The county commissioners approved Ridgway's first traffic light a few years back. It will control the traffic into a new mini mall. As might be expected, the police force is bigger, the fire truck more modern, the social services budget larger, and the taxes higher.

Fewer and fewer sons and daughters are taking over the ranches of their parents and grandparents. Inheritance taxes discourage intergenerational ranching. As the older ranchers die off or retire, their ranching skills are not passed to a younger generation, a generation that is more and more attracted to the economic opportunities promised by the urban economy. As a consequence, the land does not receive the care and attention it once did. Irrigation ditches fall into disrepair, and weeds creep into hay meadows. And as the process of gentrification continues, fancy equestrian centers sprout up on pastures as hunters and jumpers add a different, if not foreign, dimension to the landscape and the equine population. Hummers and new-model sports cars come to outnumber pickups in the parking lots of the town's two banks.

Yet for all the local efforts to enhance economic development and create jobs, there remains a keen awareness among the majority of residents that the county's most valuable resource is its natural beauty, an irreplaceable resource that needs to be nurtured and protected. The tourists who motor through the county support a vibrant summer economy. And new residents seek the visual beauty and outdoor amenities of uncluttered mountains.

These new residents have carried with them the expectation of urban amenities; clearly a new library and medical center have improved the quality of living in Ridgway. The high school now under construction will relieve crowding at the older facility. Our roads, even the many dirt ones, are better maintained. New restaurants have diversified the chicken-fried steak offerings, and satellite television has supplied new topics for conversation at the coffee shops and post office.

It is not easy to write about one's town and its people. It is not for lack of information that the task is made more difficult, but quite the opposite—too much information, sometimes of a personal nature. As a resident of Ouray County, I claim to be no authority, only one of its participants and observers. What is evident about Ouray County is its struggle to absorb new residents while coming to grips with a tourist economy often at odds with a traditional agricultural way of life. Yet for all of the internal debates—sometimes dissention—there remains a strong belief among both older residents and newcomers that they can influence the vital decisions affecting the county and hence their lives. Democracy continues to thrive in Ouray County, but it sure can be noisy from time to time.

Acknowledgments

For the historical chapters (chapters 1–3), the most useful sources were local newspapers: the *Ouray Times, Ouray County Plaindealer*, and the *Ridgway Sun*. For demographic materials, particularly regarding ethnicity and occupational information, I used the U.S. and Colorado censuses for 1880, 1890, and 1900. I am also indebted to P. David Smith's two local histories: *Ouray, Chief of the Utes* (Ridgway, 1986) and *Ouray, a Quick History* (Fort Collins, 1996), and to Doris Gregory's *Ridgway, the Town That Refused to Die* (Ouray, 1996) and Dona M. Freeman's two ranch biographies, *Smith Ranch* and *Last Dollar Ranch*, privately printed in Montrose, Colorado, in 1992 and 1993 respectively. Useful reminiscences of the county can be found in *The Way It Was* (Ridgway, 1987), by Todd Bacigalupi and David Bachman, *Ranching History of Ouray County*, 2 vols. (Ridgway, 2005), by Virginia Harrington, and *A Ranching Legacy* (Montrose, 2005), by Rafael Routson.

Readers interested in Ouray's current population trends, land ownership patterns, demographics, master plan (including zoning regulations), and calendar of events should visit the county's Web site at www.co.ouray.co.us.

Parts of chapter 4 appeared in a different form in the *Massachusetts Review* (vol. 23, no. 3, Autumn 1982) and *Northern Lights* (vol. 3, no. 1, January–February 1987). Parts of chapter 5 appeared in *Northern*

Lights (vol. 2, no. 2, March–April 1986).

The photographs were assembled from the collections of the Denver Public Library and the Ridgway Public Library (Ouray County Ranching Project). I wish to thank Barbara McCullar for her assistance with the latter collection.

Many people assisted me with information, reminiscences, and anecdotes about Ridgway and the area, past and present. Of particular assistance were Ted Collin, Roger Noble, Ed and Linda Ingo, Faye Wolford, Duane Wilson, Larry Luke, Manny and Annette Monserrate, Jean and Jeannie Brown, Mario Zadra, Ken Sodowsky, Steve Arnold, Virginia Harrington, Esther Lewis, Denise Adams, and Wilma, Mike, and Henry Potter. I absolve them, of course, of all responsibility for any errors of fact and interpretive use of the valuable information they provided.

As always, it is a delight to conduct research at the Denver Public Library, particularly the assistance of the professional staff in the Western History Room: Barbara Walton, Philip Panum, and Bruce Hanson.

Kai Erikson, Anne Price, William deBuys, Ted Moews, Bill Adler, Fred Turner, Dan Pike, Bill Silberstein, and Rich Tisdel read earlier drafts of the book and provided helpful suggestions and corrections. All writers should have the good fortune that I've had to work with Mindy Conner as a copy editor and Faith Marcovecchio, who oversaw the reprint.

I'd like to recognize both the National Endowment for the Humanities and the Rockefeller Foundation. Many years ago, they allowed me the opportunity to take time off from my university responsibilities to research some of the themes discussed in this book. That a small portion of the Rockefeller grant may have gone to purchase a cow or two in addition to its intended purpose of researching a book on the transformation of rural America will not, I hope, discourage the foundation in the future from making grants to those living and working on farms or ranches.

Finally, several people deserve special mention. My children—Karen, Christopher, and Hilary—have worked long and sometimes painful hours to help support the operation of our family ranch. And Deedee, my ranch partner and wife, was present, as always, with her constant support and love.

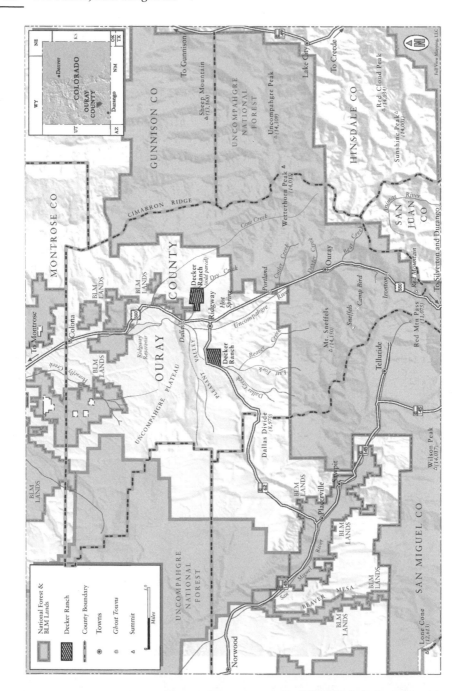

Introduction

There are few places in the American West more isolated than Ouray (pronounced u-RAY) County, Colorado. Even by the standards of the rural West, it is a difficult place to reach. Tucked away in the high country of the San Juan Mountains in the southwestern quadrant of the state, the county is close to no major interstate, has neither an airport nor an airstrip, and cannot boast a TV station, movie theater, bus stop, auto dealership, or even a single traffic light. The first fast food establishment arrived in 1994. To reach Ouray County, you have to study your map as you drive your car—carefully.

Unlike many other western counties, Ouray County cannot boast that it is home to a significant regional or national tourist attraction—not a monument or national park, not even a battlefield. No major or minor historical event that helped to shape the nation or the West ever occurred there. Hollywood has used the county's backdrop to further its own version of western history even though Butch Cassidy left the county banks alone (he did hit one in nearby Telluride), and no gunfights at high noon, or any other time, ever disturbed the place.

Some relatively well-known people have lived in Ouray County, and quite a few have visited or passed through it; but no president, no actor, no famous American was born in the county or grew up there, except maybe for "Smoky Joe" Wood. But you have to be a baseball

fan with a good memory to recognize that name. Smoky Joe moved
to the county from Kansas City with his parents at the turn of the century and at the age of fourteen was the youngest member of the town's
1904 baseball team ("assistant pitcher" and team mascot). He gained
national recognition when, in 1912, he set an American League pitching
mark with a 34–5 record (including sixteen consecutive wins and thirty-
five complete games) and led the Boston Red Sox to a World Series
championship with three wins over John McGraw's New York Giants.

In addition to its lack of notoriety, Ouray County is also, by western standards, small in both size and population. Most American cities
(and even a few Texas ranches) encompass a larger area than Ouray's
540 square miles. Of that area, about 53 percent, or 185,000 acres, is
privately owned and is home to approximately three thousand people.
The remaining 162,000 acres are either federal government lands (U.S.
Forest Service and Bureau of Land Management) or belong to the state
of Colorado. Today, fewer people live in the county's valleys than live in
a single New York City block. Livestock outnumber people by more
than three to one, and elk and deer by twice that ratio. For this reason
alone some folks find it an attractive place to live and raise a family.

Like so many residents of the American West, I came to the region
from the East. My attraction to Ouray County and its people was a
part of my attraction to the West. In my youth, I sometimes visited relatives in the West, and for three summers I worked on a sheep and cattle
outfit (now part of Ted Turner's much larger buffalo ranch) in the
mountains south of Bozeman, Montana, and just north of Yellowstone
Park in the Gallatin Valley. I hired on as a neophyte horse wrangler, but
two weeks into my first summer I was "promoted" to what is known
on a sheep ranch as a "camp Jack." I was the lowest form of life
allowed to exist on this outfit of seventy horses, 250 cows with calves,
four hundred yearling steers, and six thousand "woolies."

My job was to pack up a string of ornery horses every Sunday
afternoon and head out alone into the high country with a week's

supply of food, medicine, and provisions for two isolated sheep camps, each at timberline in the shadow of the Spanish Peaks. Over the course of those three summers, I came to know well the sheep business and the Gallatin National Forest. I learned quickly, for example, that sheep wake up every day trying to figure out a new way to die, and by evening have unlocked yet another quick pathway to death. With close to two thousand miles under my saddle, I came to know every drainage, fishing hole, open park, and mountain peak in the Gallatin Valley. After a two- or three-day ride, I'd pull into a sheep camp where the herder would barely acknowledge my arrival except to bark some orders to his newly arrived slave.

In my second summer, Tony, a bearded, fiftyish misanthrope herder who possessed all the personal charm, and aroma, of a grizzly bear, became enraged that I had brought him only a pint of blackberry brandy. He knew as well as I the supreme and illegal effort I'd made at age seventeen to purchase the pint at the Gallatin Gateway general store—and with my own meager wages. No matter. As a penalty for not arriving in camp with a quart of Four Roses whiskey, Tony's drink of choice, he pointed to a dead grizzly bear that hung from a tree out behind his camp tent in a small spruce grove and said: "Skin it." As an afterthought he added, "And don't be worrying about the maggots." Not even Tony's two scruffy sheepdogs were interested in getting close to this bloated and ripe grizzly. I wanted to say that skinning bears wasn't part of my job description, but I thought better of it as Tony scowled first at the pint of brandy, then at me, and finally at his skinning knife. Tony slung the knife at me, and, without cutting my hand or severing a finger, I caught it by the bone handle and proceeded, as if I knew what I was doing, to cut into the belly of the beast. There's not much that can compare in smell with the decomposed insides of a 450-pound grizzly left hanging in the sun for four days. I did manage, with some grumbled hints from my mentor, to detach the skin from the bloody carcass; but I never did come to appreciate the culinary delights of a greasy grizzly steak.

Those summers on horseback in the Gallatin Range imbued me with a love of the mountains, flora, and wildlife of the West (although not necessarily of its grizzly bears or sheep, and certainly not their herders). Over the years, I hiked, fished, and skied the Sierra Nevada, the Tetons, the Big Horns, the Absarokas, and the Wind River range; helped friends on their cattle ranches in Wyoming, Nevada, Texas, and Montana; and always dreaded having to leave the region and return to a dreary office back East.

I first visited Colorado in the winter of 1970. On a drive across the country from New York to San Francisco, I took a detour with a friend to head down into the San Juan Mountains of southern Colorado. I'd never been into the southern Rockies, and on the map it looked like interesting country and a good place for a couple of days of cross-country skiing.

We came into the San Juans from the south, not an easy route, particularly in the winter. A huge mountainous mass suddenly appeared to the north where only minutes before an endless deep blue sky had dominated the landscape from east to west. Snow covered everything, including the trees at lower elevations and even the brick-red rock ledges. I could see the winds blowing small blizzards of snow on peaks that broke above 12,000 feet. In a car without chains or four-wheel drive, we climbed slowly but steadily into the heart of the mountains, past cattle feeding on flakes of hay along the Dolores River, up into the old deserted mining town of Rico with its elegant but abandoned courthouse, and then on over Lizard Head Pass at 10,200 feet into the old mining town of Telluride. Here, in a town famous in the late nineteenth century for its rich gold and silver deposits, scruffy miners mixed with an even scruffier collection of hippies, who, I learned, found in this isolated mountain hideaway a comfortable counterculture refuge. We had a meal at a local café where a miner told us that the Idarado mine, the largest employer in town, was about played out and would probably soon close. We continued to head toward Ouray County, and at the county line on Dallas Divide we stopped to take in the magnificent view of the mountains back to the south and east and the snow-covered valleys below.

It was, I said to myself and to my friend, the perfect place to cross-country ski—superb fresh snow, open slopes that climbed gently toward aspen groves and, at a slightly higher elevation, stands of gigantic spruce. In one stand of aspen, we scared up a small herd of bedded elk that ran off toward the Mount Sneffels Wilderness. We skied until darkness turned the snow to gray powder under a deep purple sky. Then, exhausted, we drove off Dallas Divide and down into the tiny and rather sleepy town of Ridgway, found an inexpensive (and cold) room at the Bunk House Lodge, and dined on chicken-fried steak at the Little Chef café. It was one of those days that live forever in memory.

Four years later, I was looking to buy a small ranch. I had northern Wyoming in mind, but I couldn't afford anything I liked there; the few ranches I could afford, I didn't like. A cousin suggested I look in Colorado, specifically the southwest region, down near Telluride in a small town by the name of Ridgway. Did I know the area, he asked. "Sure do," I replied. "Let's go look." After poking around the Ridgway vicinity and looking at three ranches, I decided to make an offer on a ranch. By April 1974, my wife, Deedee, and I owned six hundred acres of hay meadows, benchland, and heavily timbered hillsides adjacent to Dallas Creek four miles west of Ridgway, all heavily mortgaged to a Montrose bank.

To call it a ranch is to suggest that the property was in some semblance of working order, which it most certainly was not. Half the barn roof had blown off toward Kansas; weeds and willows clogged the irrigation ditches; the fences and the corral stood up only out of habit; the meadows were sprinkled with baling wire, prairie dog holes, and about a dozen Old Crow bottles; and the domestic water supply originated, until very recently, in a stream where cattle drank and left their deposits. Even the driver of the moving van that brought our possessions out from Manhattan questioned my sanity. He sat wide-eyed in

the cab after wrestling the truck up our steep, rutted, narrow driveway
in an early May snowstorm, staring quizzically out at three outbuildings
that trembled in the face of a strong northwest wind, and asked in a
most respectful manner: "Sir, I have a question and I hope you don't
take this personally, but ... is this a move up?"

I moved to the ranch from New York City with some experience
and knowledge of cattle—but not, I soon realized, nearly as much as I
thought. Deedee and I learned by doing, by making mistakes, and by
asking helpful neighbors, most of whom were sons and daughters or
grandchildren of ranchers who had come to western Colorado eighty
years before. My neighbor Duane Wilson, a hard-twisted cowman
who'd grown up on a tough mountain ranch in the Gunnison valley,
told me it was fine to have a Ph.D., but "in this country, son, it darn
well better mean posthole digger."

For many years, I moved back and forth between our ranch and a
university teaching position back East. But I missed the ranch when I
was away, even in winter, and finally decided to quit the academy for
ranching. Why I chose to live and work in Ridgway after a short career
teaching American history and public policy is not easily and simply
explained. An academic colleague said to me as I left piedmont North
Carolina for the mountains of Colorado, "Let me see if I understand
this correctly. You're giving up a comfortable teaching position and a
career so you can spend the rest of your life freezing your ass off while
you babysit a bunch of stupid bovines."

"Well, not exactly," I responded. I wanted to live in a beautiful
place, especially in a small town, and to work for myself, with my family, and raise livestock (excluding, of course, sheep). And although I
enjoyed teaching (inside work without heavy lifting), too often I felt like
a spectator of life rather than an active participant. I much preferred
irrigating a hay meadow or riding a horse over attending interminable
curriculum committee meetings.

Not only did my academic friends fail to understand what I was doing in Colorado, my Boston in-laws were equally perplexed. I had dragged their only daughter off to the edge of civilized society, to an unknown region way, way west of the Charles River. So in 1984, in an attempt to explain to them what our lives were all about—what we did, how we did it, and what the people we ranched with in Ridgway were like—I wrote a rather long "Letter from Ridgway" and sent it to them. I also gave a copy to a visitor to our ranch, the curator of the Western History Collection at the Denver Public Library. A dozen years later, when I was visiting that library, that curator, Eleanor Gehres, now deceased, mentioned the letter to me and told me that she used part of it in the Colorado history course she taught. I'd forgotten all about the letter, asked for a copy, and reread it.

I was struck by how very much Ridgway had changed in the twelve years that had passed since I wrote the letter. I felt compelled to update and expand my "Letter from Ridgway," to bring some order and understanding to the chaotic changes that I, my family, and particularly the old-time county residents had lived through during the last quarter of a century. Hence this book, an account of Ouray County, Ridgway, and the unexpected and uninvited external forces that suddenly descended on a sleepy agricultural community where three generations of yeoman farmers and ranchers had tended to their crops and livestock through the rhythms of the seasons.

European Americans settled Ouray County only a century before Deedee and I moved onto our ranch. Children of the county's first settlers could tell us, from their own memories, the location of the Ute tribe's winter quarters and summer hunting grounds. They remembered their Indian playmates by name, knew the location of the Ute trails that are today's roads, and learned from the Indians where to hunt and when to plant.

For more than a century, agriculture (cattle primarily) and mining dominated the local economy, just as they did in many other rural counties in the Rocky Mountains West. After World War II, following a national trend, the number of county farms, ranches, and workers declined by about one-half while the size of the average ranch more than doubled to almost 2,000 acres. When we arrived in the county in the mid-1970s, the seventy or so livestock ranches in the county were, along with the mines above the town of Ouray, the predominant generators of its wealth and the workplaces of almost 15 percent of the county's 1,600 residents.

Today, fewer than 5 percent of the county's residents live or work on one of the forty operating ranches, which now average well in excess of 2,500 acres in size. Where farmers and ranchers were, at the turn of the century in Ouray County and across the nation, the first majority, by the early 1990s, they were the last minority. The Census Bureau announced a few years back that farmers (including ranchers) were no longer a "statistically significant" category and hence would no longer be counted.

But local residents had little trouble counting the ever-increasing horde of tourists or the many newcomers who took up seasonal or permanent residence in the county. Beginning in the early 1980s, Ouray County experienced a demographic and cultural invasion that radically transformed and disrupted the place and its residents. The outsiders brought with them values, lifestyles, and personal expectations never imagined, much less experienced, by the sons and daughters of the pioneers who settled the region a century earlier. When swimming pools, European sports cars, llamas, and "ranchers" clad in jogging outfits began to appear on nearby ranches, I knew the New West had arrived in the valley.

In the process of writing this book, I have come to recognize that the gradual disappearance of farms and ranches all across the United States in the last half century has been accompanied by a tendency to glorify the agrarian past, to stereotype it and imbue it with a romantic halo. So too with small-town life. We view farming and ranching as attractive endeavors because we see them as representing a simpler, less industrial, Jeffersonian era. And from the perspective of twentieth-century urban America, we like to imagine the physical and psychological comforts of living in a small, intimate community whose residents share values and mutual respect.

But the past can be an unpleasant place to visit if it doesn't conform to the present-day myths that have been created from it. Hamlin Garland, who wrote about the rural Midwest around the turn of the century, reminded his readers many years ago that "milking as depicted on a blue china plate where a maid in a flannel petticoat is caressing a gentle Jersey cow in a field of daisies, is quite unlike sitting down to the steaming flank of a stinking brindle heifer in fly time." And I suspect the same is true when it comes to the West. Consciously or subconsciously, we have all collected stereotypes of the West—when Tom Mix galloped through local movie theaters on Saturday mornings in the 1940s, followed by Roy Rogers in the 1950s and John Wayne in the 1960s, and more recently, when Billy Crystal trailed his critters through *City Slickers*. John Wayne, who came to Ridgway to make movies, defined what it meant to be a cowboy for the American public—and, unfortunately, for many in the cattle business as well. In fact, it can be said, probably without too much exaggeration, that John Wayne did for the cattle business what Sylvester Stallone did for acting. The movies and TV series created by Hollywood, with few exceptions, are very nice as entertainment, but they are a false rendering of the West, both the place and the people, then and now.

When friends from the city visit our ranch, they are surprised to learn that I do not spend my entire day in the saddle riding the range, singing "Git Along Little Dogies" in a ten-gallon hat with a six-shooter strapped to my hip. That I have to build an irrigation box, repair a tractor, or take my daughter to the doctor comes as something of a surprise to residents of New York, Boston, and even Denver. Some are also astounded to learn that not all Indians live on reservations, that most cowboys are little more than underpaid hourly wage earners with big hats, and that few ranch owners believe coyotes are cute.

Some of the myths of the West that we carry in our cultural baggage die hard; others refuse to die at all. Some of the myths are innocent and benign, causing a few laughs but no injury. There are, however, commonly held stereotypes about the West and its people that do cause damage. People perceived only through a misty cloud of romantic Hollywood claptrap cannot be real. Their work is portrayed by Hollywood as a form of play or recreation, so that whatever problems they suffer are somehow insignificant or imagined. The problems that afflict the rest of the world tend not to apply to our romanticized subjects. It simply cannot be possible, we are led to believe, for anyone living in a movie-set beautiful rural setting—a "little house on the prairie"—to suffer from alcoholism, a debilitating accident, or bankruptcy. In short, we in the West are all too often enthralled by our own myths.

———•••———

What follows is a partial biography of a remote place—Ouray County, Colorado—some of its history and the history of livestock ranching, and the recent changes that have come to transform the area. This book is not intended to be a definitive history but rather a long essay on what happened to a small rural county when it was confronted by what longtime residents called "an invasion of outsiders."

In a sense, I am an invader, too—I was born outside the county and have been a resident for only a quarter of a century. At the same time, as a rancher, I've been engaged in the work that until very recently defined the character and landscape of the county. It is from both perspectives that this book is written.

Chapter One

Beginnings

Western Colorado is a young country with a short history. New England was a flourishing and well-settled region long before the western frontier evolved from wilderness to statehood. It took almost two and a half centuries for Anglo settlers to move out of New England, across the fertile valleys of the Midwest, and out into the high plains and mountains of the Rocky Mountain West. Most of Thomas Jefferson's Louisiana Purchase, of which most of Colorado was a part, did not attain territorial status for an entire generation after the Civil War. In fact, most of the Rocky Mountain region, including western Colorado (acquired in the Mexican War in 1848), remained virtually empty, part of the Great American Desert, unmapped and even unexplored (with the major exception of the mining regions) until late in the nineteenth century.

The area that eventually came to be known as Ouray County was not a particularly comfortable place to live. Situated astride the San Juan Mountains at an average elevation of more than seven thousand feet, the ground was covered by snow for about half the year; the growing season never exceeded one hundred days, and the only productive soils were in the few valleys, which formed only about 10 percent of the county's area. In addition, its location on the western side of the Rockies made the county impossible to reach except by wagon from the north. The trip over the Continental Divide from the east was as difficult as it was dangerous, even in the best weather. And once over one of the three rough mountain passes (all above ten thousand feet) that led to the western slope, travelers found only primitive trails used by the region's resident population, the Ute Indians, who, although not warlike, were by no means an enthusiastic welcoming committee.

The Uncompaghre Utes and two other mountain bands were themselves relative newcomers to the area. In the seventeenth century, they had been pushed from the eastern plains into the valleys of the San Juans by the Arapaho and Cheyenne, with whom the Utes did constant battle—and usually lost. The mountain Utes, who never numbered more than four thousand, lived peacefully and undisturbed in the lower valleys of the San Juans, sheltered from the harsh snowstorms that began each October and sometimes piled as much as thirty feet of snow on the higher elevations. The Utes occupied the mountains only in the summer months, and then only the most accessible valleys.

The Franciscan Fathers Domínguez and Escalante, searching for an easy overland route from Santa Fe to the Spanish missions in California in 1776, led an expedition through the area and reported the treacherous and uninviting terrain. Seasonal trappers, mostly French and Spanish, hunted the valleys of the San Juans for beaver and deer, but only as a last resort.

Through most of the nineteenth century, the San Juans lay unexplored, unmapped, and to a large extent unknown. The closest Anglo settlement prior to the opening of the mines was that of a Quebec Frenchman named Antoine Robideaux, who in the 1820s built a trading post (Fort Uncompaghre) on the Gunnison River near present-day Delta, Colorado, to serve the Utes of the Uncompaghre Valley. Members of the Gunnison Expedition in 1853 explored and mapped the region, but their reports, like those of the Spanish fathers before them, did not describe an inviting landscape.

The Spanish, in their interminable search for silver, are thought to have come up the Rio Grande from the south to its headwaters in the

San Juans and crossed over the Continental Divide just south of
Ouray near present-day Silverton. Here they discovered silver deposits
in the mountains they called Sierra de la Plata (the Silver Mountains).
The mountains continued to be called by their Spanish name well after
the United States took possession of the area from Mexico in 1848.
Americans quickly learned from the Spanish and the Mexicans the location of the silver deposits at the headwaters of the Rio Grande, and in
the early 1850s, if not sooner, began filtering into the San Juans.

The first Anglo residents in Ouray County concerned themselves
not with the weather or the surface soils or the difficulties of surface
travel, however, but with mining the silver in the mountain lands used
for summer hunting by the Tabeguache Utes, a small band who made
their winter headquarters near present-day Montrose along the Uncompaghre (Hot Springs) River.

Whenever the Utes and the relatively few Anglo miners and trappers in the region came into contact in the nineteenth century, they left
each other alone. There was space enough for all, and neither sought
to capture what the other sought—the Utes' game or the miners' silver.
In the one recorded instance where the Utes and Anglos collided, in the
1850s, the Utes burned Fort Uncompaghre. The Anglos tended to treat
the Utes with a bit more forbearance than was given to the Arapaho to
the east and the Cheyenne to the north, tribes with a well-deserved reputation for brutal attacks on immigrants into the Colorado Territory.

It was the miners moving into Wyoming, Montana, and the
Dakota Territories who were at the root of the Indian Wars on the
northern Great Plains. In an effort to make peace and give American
miners access to new mining fields, President Ulysses S. Grant signed
the Treaty of 1868, which incidentally guaranteed possession of the San
Juan Mountains to the Utes in Colorado Territory. Not long afterward,
however, reports of more silver and some gold began to filter out of the
small mining camps at Silverton and Lake City. The Utes complained to
the federal government in Washington that the miners were invading

their land; the miners responded with demands that the Indian lands be transferred to United States ownership. Further, the miners said, to ensure the peace and safety of the region, the Indians should be removed, forcibly if necessary.

Whenever it decided to violate provisions of an Indian treaty, the United States government usually made additional promises of compliance, bought off the Indians with cash and supplies, or used military force. In its dealings with the Utes, the government used all three approaches. The government first promised to remove the miners from the region but quickly recognized that it was too late to control entry on, or mining in, Ute lands. Best to make a cash settlement, avoid bloodshed, and pacify those demanding the eradication of the Indians. In an 1873 treaty negotiated with Chief Ouray, the Utes agreed to give up their rights to the San Juans (approximately four million acres) in exchange for hunting rights and $25,000 a year in annuities (livestock and farming equipment) for all six bands of Utes. In addition, Chief Ouray was promised an annual government stipend of $1,000 for the next ten years. The Utes would continue to hold title to all ground west and north of the San Juans and the Uncompaghre Valley, including a four-mile strip with a sacred hot spring immediately to the north of the new mining town of Uncompaghre City, the present site of the city of Ouray. The Unitarian church, having learned in Boston that saving souls could be a profitable enterprise, sought and received the contract to feed the bodies and souls of the local Utes.

As the silver and gold deposits attracted hundreds of additional miners, so too did the attractive and fertile valley lands north of the mines, including the four-mile strip owned by the Utes. Without any military support, the Unitarian Indian agent at the Ute agency at the north end of the valley found himself powerless to evict the Anglo squatters. Meanwhile, Chief Ouray threatened violence if the government didn't honor its treaty obligations. In an attempt, no doubt, to placate the chief, the miners at Uncompaghre City renamed their small settlement after Chief Ouray and lobbied the federal government to either buy the troublesome four-mile strip and the rest of the Uncompaghre Valley or remove the heathens altogether.

An editorial published in the *Ouray Times* in the summer of 1877 called for the Indians to pack up and leave. It was "the industrious whites" who would "cultivate, improve and make valuable the land, thus adding to the prosperity of the whole country," not a few Indians who were "of no benefit to themselves or anyone else except maybe the Indian agents and government contractors." As far as the Indians' claim to the sacred hot spring north of town in the Uncompaghre Valley, the paper dismissed that as the "merest moonshine." The Indians seldom used the spring, the paper said. "The land is of no earthly use to the Indians and it is necessary to the prosperity of our section." Anticipating the no doubt violent consequences of not accepting a cash settlement for the valley land that lay immediately adjacent to the growing town of Ouray, the Ute chief in 1878 once again avoided bloodshed and took on behalf of his tribe the $10,000 offered by Washington.

The Ute community north of the Uncompaghre Valley on the White River was not so fortunate. Later that same year, the Indian agent in the area, Nathan Meeker, decided to teach the local Utes a lesson in the Christian work ethic and Anglo agriculture. When he had the Ute horse pasture plowed up and replanted with corn, the Indians responded by shooting at the plow teams. Meeker immediately asked for military support. When it arrived, the Indians countered the "invasion" with an attack of their own. They killed Meeker and six of his assistants; attacked the approaching cavalry column, killing fourteen and wounding forty-three; burned the entire white settlement; and kidnapped Mrs. Meeker, her daughter, another woman, and two children. Chief Ouray arranged a truce before further bloodshed broke out. To ensure the permanent safety of white settlers in the Uncompaghre region, the army established a cantonment (later named Fort Crawford) at the north end of Ouray County where cavalry and infantry companies, including a company of black soldiers, were headquartered.

Finally, after convincing themselves and the public that innocent whites had been "massacred by savages," the civil and military authorities acceded to the public demand that the Utes be removed from the area. The Utes were to be financially compensated and moved to fertile land at the confluence of the Gunnison and Grand (Colorado) Rivers near present-day Grand Junction or land "adjacent" to it. After tribal members had voted to approve the agreement, helped by a $2 handout to each voter from Otto Mears, a local businessman and adviser to Chief Ouray, Anglo agriculturalists discovered that the area was a bit too fertile and valuable for a band of renegades. The government decided instead to move the Utes to eastern Utah, a region rich in red sandstone and otherwise barren of vegetation or game.

Chief Ouray (center) with his sub-chiefs of the Tabeguache (Uncompaghre) Ute band, which made its home in the Montrose-Ridgway-Ouray area of southwest Colorado. Denver Public Library, Western History Collection, William Henry Jackson, photographer, #WHJ-10220

An Indian Commission appointed by President Garfield easily convinced Congress to ratify the agreement and to reimburse Mr. Mears ("The Pathfinder of the San Juans") for his timely "investment." One commission member dared to use the word *bribe*, but Congress awarded a $5,000 appropriation to Mears in recognition of his "valuable service" to the nation. It was neither the first time nor the last that Congress performed such an effortless semantic distinction. In September 1881, without their chief spokesman and strong leader, Ouray, recently dead of Bright's disease, the remaining Utes in western Colorado were forcibly escorted by a Fort Crawford military detachment to their new reservation in Utah.

In an article entitled "The Utes Have Gone," the *Ouray Times* joyfully announced that the Utes had "bid adieu to their old hunting grounds, folded up their tents, rounded up their dogs, sheep, goats, ponies and traps and took up the line of march for their new reservation, followed by General MacKenzie and his group. This is an event that has been long and devoutly prayed for by our people. How joyful it sounds and with what satisfaction one can say 'The Utes have gone.'" Once the Utes had been taken away, the United States government seized the remainder of their twelve million acres.

When Chief Ouray had negotiated the treaty giving up tribal lands in the mining district around Ouray in 1874, he told Colorado's Governor Elbert:

> I realize the ultimate destiny of my people. They will be extirpated by the race that overruns, occupies and holds our hunting grounds, whose number and force with the government and the millions behind it will in a few years remove the last trace of our blood that now remains. We shall fall as the leaves from the trees when ... winter comes, and the lands which we have roamed over by countless generations, will be given over to the miner and

the plowshare. In place of our humble teepees, the "white" man's towns and cities will appear and we shall be buried out of sight beneath the avalanche of the new civilization. This is the destiny of my people.

And as Chief Ouray had predicted, so it came to be.

With the Indian menace removed, the local paper announced that Easterners could now safely migrate to the Ouray region. The removal of the Utes, the paper told its readers, had thrown "open to the dominion of white men one of the most fertile and beautiful valleys in all Colorado, a valley that will be to those who are so fortunate as to become owners of its broad acres, a happy land of Canaan."

This new Canaan never did live up to the exaggerated expectations of the town fathers. In 1876, the year Colorado gained statehood, a mere 400 inhabitants occupied the motley collection of frame buildings, shacks, and tents in the newly incorporated town of Ouray. The town boasted a school, two hotels, a sawmill, a post office, an assay office, and many saloons and gambling houses. By 1880, the town's population had doubled, and another 1,800 individuals lived in the isolated mining camps of Sneffels, Ironton, and Red Mountain located above Ouray. As one traveled north from Ouray into the Uncompaghre Valley and the Dallas Creek and Cow Creek drainages, which fed into the Uncompaghre River, small farming and livestock operations replaced miners' cabins.

As might be expected in a newly settled mining region, the county's population was predominantly male (85 percent, according to the 1880 census) and young. The few men who moved to the county with their families lived in town. Single men lived in hotels or in one of the many boardinghouses, whose residents, not surprisingly, organized themselves by language and ethnicity. One of every five residents in the town and in the camps was foreign-born, although English was the native tongue of more than half of these. After the English, Irish, Welsh, Scots, and Canadians, Germans were the most numerous among the foreign-born.

Among the native-born, almost half had been born in the Midwest, and 15 percent came from New York (half of these were first-generation Americans, mostly of Irish descent), including the sheriff and his deputy, the county judge, and two attorneys.

With the exception of San Juan County to the south, organized around Silverton, no Colorado county was more difficult of access in the late nineteenth century than Ouray. The only reliable road in and out of Ouray County came in from the north. Once it passed through Ouray, the road dead-ended against the steep rock walls that surrounded the town like a horseshoe on three sides. A treacherous and expensive ($5 per wagon and team) toll road built by Otto Mears came into Ouray from Silverton to the south, but it was subject to avalanches and passable only about three months of the year.

Even the arrival of the Denver & Rio Grande Railroad in 1887 from the north and the improvement of the toll road from the south failed to attract the population the town boosters expected. Although Ouray's rich ore deposits and the silver boom provided the immediate wealth and resources to build a small population base and infrastructure for a county, the remote location and rough topography to a large extent defined the county's character for another century.

Despite its isolation, Ouray County reached its peak population, almost six thousand—twice its present-day size—in the early 1890s. The county boasted eight towns (Red Mountain, Ironton, Sneffels, Ouray, Portland, Ridgway, Dallas, and Colona; see map), each with its own school, shops, and primitive services. All roads, however, led to Ouray, the county seat and the region's premier town.

Before the depression of 1893 struck, there were more than ten large producing mines in the immediate vicinity of the city of Ouray (pop. 2,534 in 1890). The Revenue, Tomboy, Camp Bird, Atlas, and Virginius were world famous. Most of the mines were owned by out-of-state investors, who stayed at the elegant Beaumont Hotel when they visited Ouray.

The usual array of shops lined Main Street: hardware, clothing, bakery, pharmacy, livery stable, dry goods, and produce. The street also featured the new Opera House, the Delmonico Hotel, the newspaper office, the Masonic Lodge, and two restaurants that advertised upstairs rooms for "boarders." West of Main Street, toward the river, were the handsome new Denver & Rio Grande rail depot, additional hotels, a brewery, a freight office, and the San Juan Coal, Lumber, and Supply Company.

Interspersed between these establishments were Chinese laundries, livery stables, a blacksmith shop, boarding houses, and a two-block array of saloons with such enticing names as The Temple of Music, Monte Carlo, Bon Ton, Bucket of Blood, and The Bird Cage. For two bits, a visitor got a drink and a dance with one of the "girls on the line," most of whom had been attracted to Ouray from the East or from the other nearby mining towns of Aspen, Silverton, and Telluride. These courtesans serviced their customers either in the upstairs rooms of the saloons or at the "cribs" where they lived. The respectable citizens from uptown shunned the Second Street fleshpots and instead frequented the Western Hotel, the Elks Lodge, and the Opera House for their program dances, cheaper drinks, and better food.

Town ordinances defined acceptable behavior and the penalties for deviating from it. Privies could be transported through town only in closed containers and only in the early morning hours before sunup. Dead animals had to be removed from town within six hours of death. Weapons could be carried only for "legitimate purposes," a vague term that no doubt provided legal fodder for the town's thirteen lawyers. As for prostitution, an ordinance declared that "no bawdy house or house of ill-fame or the place for the practice of fornication shall be maintained within the limits of the town of Ouray or three miles beyond the outer limits." Clearly the ordinance was not enforced, because additional ordinances that *were* strictly enforced defined the blocks to which prostitution was confined (the "reservation") and the amount the very profitable "bawdy houses" had to pay the city for liquor licenses. When the Episcopal Church Ladies attempted to reform the town's "sinners," the local newspaper editor, known for his acerbic wit, responded in an editorial that the ladies would have more success against "miners and editors, as experience has taught ... that lawyers and bank cashiers are not worth saving."

Like all mining towns in areas with rich mineral deposits, Ouray was home to a collection of newcomers who were vague about their backgrounds. In his book *Early Days on the Western Slope*, Sidney Jocknick, an early resident, described the composition of Ouray's citizenry in the late 1870s as "men dishonorably discharged from the Army, crooks and desperadoes, and still others who had left their country for their country's good." One's past notwithstanding, it was possible in Ouray to "redeem a clouded reputation" and be "born again" with a new identity. Ouray promised settlers a new life, "a bright prospect and all the world a glorious opportunity."

Regardless of their past lives, the citizens of Ouray took pride in their town's appearance. Up the hill and east of Main Street, the town proudly displayed its new two-story schoolhouse. The interior of the six-thousand-square-foot building was elegantly trimmed with ash, oak, and walnut; the brick exterior was detailed with gray sandstone and capped off with a handsome metal hip roof with an elegant bell tower. Private subscriptions funded the miners' hospital (currently the home of the Ouray County Historical Museum), a stone structure erected next to the Catholic church that was operated by the Sisters of Mercy. The hospital was available to all miners who paid a dollar a month for emergency medical insurance. One block away sat the new brick county courthouse. Immediately to the south of the courthouse, new clapboard, brick, and stone homes replaced the original log cabins and shanties built in the 1870s. In this "respectable" neighborhood lived the mine superintendents and the new professional class (lawyers, bankers, engineers, and bookkeepers) who served the mine owners.

But it was the Beaumont Hotel, built at a cost of $85,000, that reflected both the town's new wealth and its optimism for the future. Male visitors (who included Teddy Roosevelt and Herbert Hoover) entered the brick-and-stone Victorian structure through the main gentlemen's entrance (ladies had their own entrance on a side street off Main), which led into a large, circular lobby open to the second-floor skylight. In the lobby, which featured glass display cases filled with mineral samples from local mines, were the telegraph office and front desk. Off the lobby was a parlor where a visitor might discuss a business transaction. A bar with a billiards table was adjacent to the parlor. Also on the first floor were the city's two banks (the Merchants and Miners Bank and the Bank of Ouray) and a barbershop. A solid oak stairway led to the second floor, where a walkway circled the rotunda and led to additional parlors, the spacious dining room, and the twenty-nine private hotel rooms—some with balconies overlooking the mountains to the south. The finish throughout was hardwood, and the ceiling trim was relieved with gold. On the third floor were twenty-four additional apartments, most with their own baths, and all, like the second-floor rooms, supplied with running hot water from the local mineral springs. The Beaumont's guests, who usually gave their occupations as "mine owner" or "capitalist," paid $4 a day; working-class hotels such as the Western charged $1.25 a night.

In stark contrast to the opulence of the Beaumont were the shacks and boardinghouses at the mining camps, which lacked all the amenities of civilized society. Accessible only by foot, mule, or horse over rock trails that sometimes disappeared in winter avalanches into deadly deep canyons, the camps, frequently located at elevations above eleven thousand feet, were both home and workplace for the majority of county residents in the late nineteenth century. The miners slept and ate in rough, uninsulated multilevel wooden barracks that adhered precariously to the mountainsides and were heated by wood or coal stoves. The miners stripped the adjoining hillsides of their timber for fuel or hauled coal up from Ouray on pack animals.

The Beaumont Hotel, the city of Ouray's fanciest hotel in the nineteenth century. The Gothic-style brick-and-stone hotel served as the temporary headquarters for visiting mine owners. Denver Public Library, Western History Collection, William Fick, photographer, #X-63052

That people were willing to live and work at elevations two miles above sea level in cold and treacherous conditions was testament to the lack of alternative employment at the time. Mining promised a daily wage, and with some luck maybe even a quick fortune. And no doubt for quite a few miners who would never admit it, the inaccessible mountains of southwestern Colorado also offered a hideaway from the law and past mistakes and the opportunity to start over with a new alias.

The geographical origins of the county's first generation of miners suggest that most possessed some familiarity with the rigors of mining, be it the coal mines of Pennsylvania or Wales, the hardrock mines of the European Alps, or the bogs of Ireland. There were some, of course, who came to the mines without skills and with a romantic image of a new life where instant wealth would come as easily as plucking gold flowers off a blooming bush. Even at a pay scale of $3–5 a day, it did not take long for veterans and neophytes alike to learn that hardrock mining in the San Juans was far different from working in the mines of the Dolomites or the sewers of New York City. The miners blasted tunnels to reach the rich deposits deep inside the mountains, mucked and hauled ore, and lived and worked in an environment of rockslides, avalanches, and dank boardinghouses where temperatures often dropped below zero for weeks at a time. The precise number of deaths in these camps was never documented, but it is certain that many died in avalanches, in horrendous mining accidents, and from diseases—mostly pneumonia and "consumption" (later called black lung).

When the United States Census Bureau announced in 1890 that any town with a population surpassing two thousand could declare itself a city, the Ouray Town Council proudly proclaimed, "We have advanced to the grade of city of the second class." Although it never reached Aspen's size (eleven thousand people) or annual mineral production ($10 million in 1889), Ouray's mining wealth placed it, along with Aspen, Leadville, and Cripple Creek, among the state's wealthiest mining communities.

Soon after Ouray celebrated its new status, the city was struck hard by a depression that affected the entire nation. Beginning in 1892, European markets for American exports (mostly agricultural commodities) collapsed, and European creditors dumped their American securities on the market, draining the nation of its gold. Convinced that American monetary policy was chiefly to blame for the Panic of 1893, President Grover Cleveland summoned a special session of Congress to return United States currency to the gold standard by repealing the Sherman Silver Purchase Act of 1890 and to enact legislation that would, Cleveland said, "put beyond all doubt or mistake the intention and ability of the Government to fulfill its pecuniary obligations in money universally recognized by all civilized countries"—that is, in gold.

With the Treasury Department freed of its obligation to purchase silver, the price of silver plummeted, closing mines and causing a major economic recession throughout the West. Colorado's Bureau of Labor Statistics estimated that forty-five thousand Coloradans were unemployed in the summer of 1893, including half of Ouray's male population. In addition, a local bank failed, train crews were laid off, and, in an act that symbolized the city's dismal economic condition, the Ouray Electric Light and Power Company shut off all the streetlights.

Local, state, and even national politicians promised immediate relief for the nation's silver-mining towns if the country would divorce itself from the "gold bug." One pioneer resident of Ouray who ran a livery stable thought so much of the 1896 Democratic presidential nominee, who urged the country back onto the silver standard, that he named his firstborn son William Jennings Bryan Fischer. By the turn of the century, at about the time the town's population had begun to diminish and after the Democratic standard-bearer's silver plank had been roundly defeated, the father had shortened the boy's name to just plain Bryan.

It was a sign of the poor economy when, in 1902, white Ouray laborers demanded the removal of the town's few Chinese residents, who, because they sent their earnings back home, "interfered with the possibilities ... of white labor." The Chinese refused to assimilate, the *Ouray Times* complained. They "are a class of citizens which are objectionable. ... We have no earthly use for any alien who comes to this country for no other purpose than to grab as much money [from] our people as he can and sends it forever out of the country to build and enrich some foreign population." Of course, the writer failed to recognize (or admit) that foreign investors in Ouray mines, particularly the English and many foreign-born miners, were also exporting capital outside the country.

The city of Ouray never again attained the population level or affluent comfort it achieved just before the Panic of 1893. Unlike the towns of Aspen and Creede, however, it survived the silver crisis, mainly because its ore had always carried a small percentage of gold. The county's mines tripled their production of gold between the mid-1890s and 1900. And with the arrival of the railroad in 1887, lower-grade concentrate could be profitably shipped to smelters in western Colorado or Denver. As the more accessible surface veins played out in the late nineteenth century, the mining industry required more and more capital to both discover and recover the rich ores hidden deep within the interior of the San Juans. Large consolidated mining corporations financed by eastern and European investors replaced the small, undercapitalized mining partnerships of the 1880s and early 1890s, and increasingly, decisions affecting the operation of the mines were made outside the county.

With the introduction of new mining techniques and machinery, especially pneumatic drills, and electricity to the mines early in the twentieth century, many miners found themselves without jobs. Others had to give up the mines for health reasons. There was no water available to retard the dust from the air drills (the miners called them "widow makers"), and an increasing number of men contracted silicosis, or "rock in the box." Some miners migrated to the rich silver and gold deposits in Montana and Idaho, and a few took up farming and ranching on homesteads in the valley and on the mesas north of Ouray.

As the nineteenth century came to a close, mining defined the character of the county. Austrian, Italian, Swedish, German, and Irish immigrants, along with young miners from Pennsylvania and farm boys from the Midwest, had extracted well over $100 million in rich ore from beneath the ground's surface. The city of Ouray, carved out of Ute lands, was recognized as one of the richest mining settlements in the entire West.

In 1900, the county was home to 4,731 residents. Compared with 1880, when only one of every five Ouray town residents was foreign-born, in 1900, one-third had been born overseas. Swedes and Italians in equal numbers made up 40 percent of the town's foreign-born population. In the mining camps outside Ouray, the foreign-born made up about half the population, although in some mines, like the Revenue in the town of Sneffels, four of every five miners had been born overseas. The skilled workers (machinists, bookkeepers, and engineers) and the higher-paid day laborers were predominantly native-born Americans, and the lower-paying unskilled jobs (ore sorters, miners) went to recently arrived immigrants from Austria, Italy, and Sweden. Austrians and Italians, all from the Tyrolean Alps, made up the vast majority of the foreign-born population in Sneffels and a somewhat smaller percentage of the mining camps of Red Mountain, Imogene, and Ironton.

At the end of the nineteenth century, Ouray County's high country looked very much as it had when the Indians left it: a mountainous terrain eroded by a series of lush interconnected river valleys, with giant cottonwoods growing along the waterways adjacent to rich grass meadows, giving way at the higher elevations to open mesas and wooded hillsides of juniper, piñon, sage, and brush oak. The mining left some scars—shafts and tailings pockmarked barren hillsides cut clean of timber—but the mines and their aboveground buildings occupied less than 1 percent of the county's area.

Fish and wildlife were abundant. Cutthroat, brook, brown, and rainbow trout, even the rare golden variety, thrived in the county's rivers, streams, and lakes. For centuries, hunters had lived off the rich variety of game birds, including quail, doves, ducks, geese, and grouse. Hawks, vultures, and eagles scoured the valleys for prey. Marmots and mountain sheep lived in the higher elevations, above the elk, deer, black bears and grizzlies, mountain lions, bobcats, lynx, and porcupines. In the valleys were turkeys, badgers, prairie dogs, squirrels, skunks, and rabbits. The streambeds, with their lush assortment of willows and alders, were home to beavers, muskrats, and native trout.

The beauty of Ouray County was not lost on the local residents in the nineteenth century, or on outsiders, who in growing numbers came to visit and live there in the twentieth century.

Chapter Two

Pioneer Settlers

One of America's defining characteristics, particularly for Westerners, is the geographical mobility of its population, both native-born residents and immigrants from other countries. The Smith brothers, who migrated to Ouray County in the late 1870s, typify the movements made by many individuals before they settled down and formed permanent roots.

Oscar and James Smith came into the Uncompaghre Valley hoping to establish themselves in the stock-raising business. Born in British Canada, they had departed for the United States separately, leaving at home their parents and a younger brother and sister. Oscar, born in 1836, went to Iowa in 1854 and then to Denver in 1855. He mined for a while, apparently without success, before making four trips back across the Great Plains and, in the late 1860s, spending three years in Montana. In the early 1870s, Oscar met up with his brother James in the San Luis Valley of southern Colorado. With their English brides and four small children, the Smith brothers migrated north into the vicinity of the Wet Mountains, where they tried their luck at farming and stock raising.

In 1879, the Smiths moved once again, this time to the Western Slope of Colorado, where the mines were generating a demand for fresh food, particularly beef. The Smith brothers and their families first settled— squatted, actually—on Indian land north of Ouray, and later, when the Ute lands were opened for settlement, moved to a site on the Uncompaghre

River near present-day Colona at the northern end of Ouray County where they remained. In the absence of a land office, they took up residence on a small but fertile floodplain that sat protected on the river by high rock cliffs. With knowledge gained from their attempts to raise stock in the cold and windy San Luis Valley near Alamosa, they carefully chose a homestead site that would provide protection for their livestock from Colorado's fierce winter snowstorms.

Like the Smiths, other young men, some also with families, began to move into the Uncompaghre Valley and the smaller Cow Creek and Dallas Creek valleys north of Ouray. After the Ute land claims were settled and the tribe removed to Utah and southern Colorado, small subsistence farms and ranches began to appear in the area. Eventually they would serve a mining area that extended from Ouray over into the Telluride region and beyond to the new mines at Rico. One newcomer to the region exclaimed: "There's so much growin' in this country you can make a living by accident."

Native-born Americans and immigrants alike were attracted to the region by the prospect of free land offered under the provisions of the Homestead Act of 1860. Those who came from the Midwest called themselves sodbusters, but the already established cattlemen in the area referred to them as "damned nesters" or "squatters." The Utes had a name for them, too, which, literally translated, means "maggots." The federal government sanitized them with the title "homesteaders." It was all part of what the American historian Gary Wills called "the great urge of the American imagination … to light out for the territory." Attracted to the American West by the exaggerated, if not completely false, advertisements of the railroads and land companies with their visions of a bountiful tomorrow, the settlers came, leaving behind debts, broken families, poverty, boredom, and even prison sentences.

Prospective farmers and stockmen traveled into the county with their two most valuable possessions: their youth and a good team of horses. Some also brought along a plow, seeder, butter churn, rifle, some basic tools, and a few animals. Most came by way of Gunnison over Blue Mesa Summit (the early settlers called it "Son of a Bitch Hill") and Cerro Summit. After a stopover in Montrose for supplies, they would proceed up the Uncompaghre Valley searching for a farm site on level ground with winter protection, decent soil, and a good water source.

The first settlers of Ouray County were not eastern capitalists looking for adventure or remittance men from wealthy European families seeking a fortune in a new country; nor were the majority refugees from the nation's booming cities. For the most part, they were either men who came out to Colorado to work in the mines or around them as freighters, horse traders, or railroad workers, or farmers from eastern and midwestern farms that could no longer support them. The farm boys knew something about growing crops but not much about ranching at a high altitude in a cold climate. Working-class people, they were accustomed to living on the margins, a background that would stand them in good stead in the years to come. Buoyed by expectations generated by the railroad advertisements, they carried with them excitement and hopes for a new and better life.

Filing a claim at the land office in Montrose made a homesteader the proud owner of a minimum of 160 acres—after making the prescribed minimal improvements, paying a modest fee, and living on the property for five years. If family members filed claims on adjoining land, a not uncommon practice, the homestead might grow to a full section (640 acres). Ranchers frequently made it a condition of employment for a hired man that he file on a quarter or half section, which, when "proved up," was to be transferred to the employer. Some homesteaders chose to bypass the residency and improvement requirements by paying $1.25 an acre and taking immediate title to the property. Civil War veterans were allowed to count their years of service toward the five-year residency requirement.

Western Colorado was something of a homesteading backwater.

More fertile, temperate, and accessible farm- and ranchlands were available in Kansas, Nebraska, the Dakotas, and along the eastern side of the Rockies in Montana, Wyoming, and Colorado. There wasn't much land suitable for homesteading in southwestern Colorado, especially in the San Juans, and the expense of moving there, as measured against the ease with which a homesteader could travel into western Kansas or eastern Colorado, further mitigated against a massive influx of homesteaders into the Uncompaghre Valley. In fact, those already settled in the area (miners, freighters, and farmers) filed on more Ouray County homestead sites than did newcomers. Many of the migrants who came into the area from other parts of the United States and from Canada, Western Europe, and the British Isles were probably attracted as much by letters from relatives already established in the region as by promotional literature circulated in their hometowns by the railroads and land companies.

The majority (60 percent) of the first generation of homesteaders were native-born Americans, primarily from the Midwest; of the foreign-born, most were British Canadians or Europeans. Most new settlers reached Ouray County through a series of circuitous moves, exemplified by those of John Kettle, an Englishman born in 1835. With the assistance of Mormon missionaries, Kettle left his family and home in Lincolnshire, according to his granddaughter Faye Wolford, "to get away from the lords and the earls" and start a new life in the United States. Kettle sailed on the *Clara Wheeler* from Liverpool and arrived in New Orleans late in the summer of 1854. He proceeded up the Mississippi to St. Louis, and then on to Omaha. From there, in 1855, he traveled west to Salt Lake City with an emigrant train.

The next year, his parents left Lincolnshire for the United States with the rest of the family and traveled west to meet John in Utah. The senior Kettles joined a Mormon handcart company in Iowa City, Iowa, and headed for Salt Lake under the direction of Captain Edmund Ellsworth. The company left Iowa on June 9, 1856, with 273 people, well over half of whom were women and children. Within a month, 33 had dropped out. Twelve died along the way, including a small baby, a young man who "expired of quick consumption," a man who was killed by lightning, and another young man who succumbed to diarrhea. Captain Ellsworth's journal entry for September 6–7 notes: "Spent all day looking for lost cattle. Sept. 7: left 7:30 A.M. Traveled 22 Miles, roads good first 14 miles, last [roads] sandy and heavy. Camped at 6:30 P.M. on Sweetwater. George Neappris died, Age 24. (Named Sweetwater because [we] lose a mule loaded with sugar)." Nineteen days later, Governor Brigham Young greeted the wagon train outside Salt Lake, and the next day, young John Kettle and his father, mother, and six siblings, aged two through eighteen, were reunited.

The Kettle homestead in Ouray County. The family had moved to Colorado in the 1880s as disenchanted exiles from Brigham Young's experiment in the Utah desert. Ranching History of Ouray County of the Ridgway Public Library

The Kettle family farmed near Salt Lake for fourteen years; they helped lay the cornerstones for the Mormon Tabernacle. In 1870, the year John Kettle Sr. died, young John moved his mother and siblings, for reasons unknown, to Westcliff, Colorado, at the edge of the Wet Mountains at the north end of the San Luis Valley. John, now the head of an eight-member family, hired on with a local cattle outfit as a cowboy, spent 1877–78 in Kansas, and then returned to Westcliff, where he remained for another nine years. In 1887, he moved his family to Colona, attracted there, no doubt, by his brother-in-law Oscar Smith, who had married John's oldest sister when he too worked in the Westcliff area. In 1880, the census taker in Colona counted four English-born families (the Middletons, Kettles, Collins, and Eldridges) and two from British Canada; half of them had emigrated to Colorado as exiles from Brigham Young's experiment in the Utah desert.

Not all of the pioneer ranchers and farmers started out wanting a life on the soil or with an attraction to the Mormons. Edwin Fischer migrated to the county from a small town in Illinois to escape the Mormon religion. Fischer operated a livery stable in Ouray before taking up ranching near Ridgway, a new rail town ten miles north of Ouray, and marrying the daughter of William Bruce Phillips, an English-born Ridgway rancher. Phillips had himself given up his occupation in England as a gleaner to seek a new life in the United States with his young bride. He went to Utah with a Mormon wagon train, but he became disenchanted with the Mormon religion. Fischer's grandson, Ed Ingo, learned from his relatives that Ouray County settlers in the 1870s and 1880s "either couldn't speak English, or sounded like they came from the wrong side of London."

One Englishman who did speak the King's English, Richard Collin, the grandson of Lord Nelson and the middle son of an Essex County vicar, sought a better future for himself, if not a fortune, in the Ouray mines. After a mine accident blinded him in one eye, he took up cattle farming in the Colona area on land adjacent to other English-born

settlers. Otto Von Hagan emigrated to Ridgway's Pleasant Valley from
Germany with his wife, daughter, and four sons. The two oldest boys
worked for their father as laborers while the two younger sons attended
school with their sister. George Hastings of New York staked out a
homestead on a barren and rather bleak mesa on the west side of Dallas
Divide that would eventually carry his name. Some farmers held down
several jobs. In addition to running a small farm on the outskirts of
Ridgway, Thomas Herran of Ohio was listed in the 1880 Census as a
miner, meat cutter, and wheelwright.

The creation of the town of Ridgway resulted from two events that
occurred within eighteen months of each other. First, a devastating fire
in 1888 destroyed much of Dallas, a small trading town on the Uncompaghre River. A year later, Otto Mears, the local entrepreneur who had
negotiated the Utes' withdrawal from the San Juans, organized a new
railroad, the Rio Grande Southern, to serve the expanding San Juan
mining district. Built with income derived from toll roads he had built
through the San Juans, government mail and beef contracts, and the
assistance of outside investors, Mears's narrow-gauge line, completed in
1890, connected the Denver & Rio Grande railroad on the Uncompaghre
River with the mining towns of Telluride, Rico, Dolores, and Durango—
a total of 162 miles of new railroad. For topographical reasons, the Rio
Grande Southern line took off from the Denver & Rio Grande at a site
two miles south of the burned-out shell of Dallas. The new railroad
immediately called the junction site Ridgway, after Colonel Robert
"Old Tige" Ridgway, a New Jersey–born engineer who gained his railroad experience in the East, including with the Union Army, and later
worked for the Kansas Pacific Railroad and the Denver & Rio Grande
before becoming superintendent of the Rio Grande Southern Construction Company.

The Ridgway Townsite Company, organized by Mears and designed
to profit from the existence of the railroad, bought up all the land at
Ridgway Junction (almost six hundred acres) from local farmers. Mears

brought three additional primary investors into the land company: Dewitt Clinton Hartwell, a transplanted New Englander, Ouray entrepreneur (the Beaumont Hotel), and investor and board member of the Rio Grande Southern; Charles H. Nix, a German investor from Chicago with experience in building and running hotels; and Frederick Walsen, another German who helped finance other Mears projects, including toll roads and a freight company.

From its inception, Ridgway was a rail town. Passengers and freight either continued up-valley to Ouray from there or changed to the narrow-gauge Rio Grande Southern for the trip over Dallas Divide (8,970 feet) to Telluride, then over Lizard Head Pass (10,222 feet) to Rico, Dolores, and Durango. Repair and machine shops and a roundhouse defined the small town's southern edge; west of the tracks were a hotel, bank, railroad office (the Mears Building), general store, newspaper office, grocery store, coal shed, icehouse, boardinghouse, and several saloons.

Ridgway served as the rail terminus for the narrow-gauge Rio Grande Southern railroad, which served the mining district to the west. Until the advent of improved road transportation in the 1930s, the railroad was the primary carrier for ore from the local mines and livestock off the regions' farms and ranches. Denver Public Library, Western History Collection, Otto Perry, photographer, #OP-14650

The pride of Ridgway, however, was the new railroad depot, built at a cost of $5,000 in 1890. The depot opened with a gala ball. The *Ridgway Herald*, in the typical boomtown language of the day, proudly reported the building to be "a large, commodious and handsome one, elegantly finished inside and out … the pride and joy of this booming burg."

First the local blacksmith shop and then the unfinished kitchen of the town's newest hotel served as the town's school before a two-story brick school building was erected in 1892. The Ridgway Townsite Company donated the land and helped finance the $10,000 construction bond issue. With their first priority completed, the newly elected town trustees organized a government, elected officers (including the town's first mayor, Charles W. Gibbs, a civil engineer from Maine employed by the railroad), and immediately defined misdemeanors, vagrancy, nuisances, and other public offenses. And to further demonstrate to the residents of this frontier town that law and order would prevail, the trustees four days later authorized the construction of a town hall (the "temple of justice") and a jail. The income needed to run the jail and pay a schoolteacher and the part-time mayor came from operating licenses issued to saloons, hotels, and restaurants. In addition, the town trustees listened to (and sometimes acted on) public complaints about sidewalks, street repairs, water rates, and stray dogs.

About the time Ridgway organized itself into an incorporated town and the railroad line to Durango was nearing completion, the Panic of 1893 struck. Building site sales and construction came to a halt in Ridgway, and late in the summer of 1893, the Rio Grande Southern, Otto Mears's railroad, filed for bankruptcy. The Bank of Ridgway survived the panic, but the Methodist Episcopal Church did not; it was sold at public auction to two enterprising residents who tore down the wooden structure and used the lumber to build their private residences. The Ridgway Townsite Company, like the bank, survived thanks to the direction of frugal Amos Walther, a man whose astute leadership brought Ridgway through the difficult times.

By the turn of the century, Ridgway was a small but thriving town with a resident population of 245 that included a wide range of skilled artisans (a bricklayer, a sawyer, 3 seamstresses, 10 carpenters, 6 teachers, 4 blacksmiths, a barber, a banker, a nurse, an attorney, and a musician), unskilled workers (3 log choppers, 3 teamsters, 10 day laborers, and 3 servants), and 38 miners who commuted to the mines above Ouray. The railroad provided about a third of the town's jobs and most of the town's tax base. Although the 1900 census taker located 37 "Courtesans" in Ouray, he found no prostitutes in Ridgway, or at least none who admitted to it. But the town was home to a fifty-eight-year-old Chinese laundry-man, Lee Choi, a resident of the United States for a quarter of a century; and a black Alabaman, born into slavery in 1852, who came to Colorado by way of New Mexico and lived with his wife and their two children above a Ridgway saloon where he worked as a porter.

The depression only temporarily halted the growth of the county's farm and ranch economy. Some whose jobs and incomes were affected by the economic slowdown in the mid-1890s—miners, freighters, saloon keepers, boardinghouse owners, and construction and rail crews—homesteaded in the valleys and on the mesas of the county. Oscar Brandt and Robert Bennett left their mining jobs in the small town of Portland, five miles south of Ridgway, and moved to homesteads on Dry Creek. Their homesteads were absorbed into a sheep ranch assembled by Juan Pouchoulou, a French Basque, in the 1940s and bought by me in 1975. In 1891, John Kettle bought a small ranch three miles west of Ridgway on Dallas Creek with the income he earned from raising and hauling oats to the mines in Ouray. John's great-grandchildren operate the ranch today.

The number of farms and ranches in the county tripled from twenty-eight to eighty-three between 1880 and 1900, and then more than doubled in the next decade. By the turn of the century, the farming population was predominantly (70 percent) native-born; as in earlier decades, more than half had been born in the Midwest. Of the foreign-born farmers and ranchers, half had been born in either England, Canada, or Germany. About half of the county's farms and ranches were owned and operated by single men like Richard Collin, the English vicar's son, who moved onto a small ranch near Colona with two Mexican laborers.

On family farms, children provided much of the labor. Typical in its household arrangement, although not necessarily its size, was the Merling farm, owned in 1880 by a sixty-one-year-old farmer who came to the United States in 1856 from Germany with his wife, Mary, age fifty-two. Merling farmed in Vermont before moving to Colorado in 1870. The Merling outfit supported John and Mary, their five sons, two daughters-in-law, and seven grandchildren, plus three boarders and the two farm laborers who worked for Merling.

A typical late nineteenth-century hardscrabble livestock ranch on Dallas Creek, west of Ridgway. Courtesy of the Colorado Historical Society, #CHSJ2017.

Living conditions on Ouray County's first farms were primitive, even by late nineteenth-century standards. The farmhouse was a hand-hewn log cabin with a dirt floor and sod roof that usually consisted of two rooms—one for cooking and eating and the other for sleeping. Nearby outside were an outhouse, crude corrals, and maybe a log shed for storing wood and sheltering animals. The cabin was located close to a well, spring, or stream.

To be productive, the land needed to be cleared of scrub oak, sage, and junipers, and irrigation ditches had to be surveyed and dug, the ground leveled, rocks removed, and the crops planted early enough to catch the first week in the ninety-day growing season yet late enough to avoid a late spring frost. The best lands at the lower elevations were given over to small grains—wheat, corn, barley, and oats—and fruit trees. Good native meadows were kept in grass and maintained for an assortment of livestock, including cattle, pigs, sheep, chickens, and a few dairy cows. The main dairy herds, however, were located up-valley, where the merchants of Ouray and the smaller mining towns required a daily supply of fresh milk, butter, and cheese.

The marginal mesa lands above the valley, where short grasses and sharp rocks competed for fifteen inches of annual moisture, were the last areas to be settled. Homesteaders there worked within a much shorter growing season, sometimes experiencing snow into late June, and maybe again as early as September. In July and August, there were hailstorms. On Hastings and Horsefly Mesas, where the high altitude and the rocky soil made growing anything but grass difficult, the open meadows were appropriate only for grazing, some potato farming, and winter wheat. Nevertheless, as much out of habit as necessity, the early homesteaders broke soils at elevations above seven thousand feet in the expectation that small grains and some vegetables would supplement their primitive livestock operations.

Homesteaders derived their income from the sale of grains, milk, cream, butter, fresh eggs, and meat (beef, venison, mutton, or pork) to the general store in town. If the store was well stocked, the farmer might trade his produce for nails, tools, seed, probably some canned goods for the winter, and necessary dry goods such as canvas pants, gloves, and waterproof boots or a heavy woolen overcoat. He also needed to replenish the homestead's supplies of salt, cloth, sugar, and coffee; sometimes he bought new barbed wire and maybe a few new tools such as an ax, plow, or hay rake. If he couldn't find what he needed in Ridgway or Colona, he went on to Montrose (either by wagon or train), or possibly as far away as Grand Junction, to purchase the necessary items with cash. Denver was a mail-order depository, too far to travel to and too expensive to visit.

Customers and employees pose inside Dr. William Rowan's Ouray Drug Store. The town's post office was located in the rear of the store. The glass cases displayed "Rat Cheese," rum, cigars, medicines, hairbrushes, and combs. Stuffed animals adorn the top of the walls. Denver Public Library, Western History Collection, #X-12662

Whatever these first primitive subsistence farmers and ranchers did not need for their own existence, they sold in the mining camps. The scarce fresh fruit grown in the Colona area commanded high prices. So too did fresh vegetables, dairy products, and eggs. Cattle, sheep, hogs, and chickens were raised on the valley farms and ranches, slaughtered and dressed, and then shipped up to the mines throughout the year. Local farms and ranches also sold feed (hay and oats) to teamsters and miners for the hundreds of pack animals that transported food, equipment, and ore in and out of the mining camps.

More than anything else, the availability of water determined the location and success of the early homesteaders. In addition to, but more important than, filing for acreage at the land office, landowners appropriated water through Colorado's early water-rights system. In the late nineteenth century, a landowner could obtain the right to use water from a stream simply by building a ditch and taking the water. Later the landowner would go to the Water Court and prove he had used a specific quantity of water (measured in cubic feet per second) for a specific purpose (irrigation) and a defined period (summer irrigation season). Once the Water Court approved the farmer or rancher's application, he could use the prescribed amount of water each summer, assuming the amount of water was available in the river or creek and that the use had commenced on a particular date, establishing a priority. The Water Court decree established, for all time, the rights of this landowner relative to others (the water right).

This system was foreign to farmers from the Midwest, East, and Europe, who were accustomed to farming in areas where the annual rainfall mostly exceeded thirty inches and there was no need to ration water. In the dry regions west of the 100th meridian (an approximate line running through the middle of the Dakotas down into Nebraska, Kansas, the Oklahoma panhandle, and on into central Texas), however, strict laws governed the use of water. Where in the East water may be taken by a property owner from a stream or river simply because it passes through his or her property, in the dry regions of the West the landowner can withdraw only the amount specified in his or her water right for use on a specific piece of land.

In this semidesert climate, where precipitation averaged only seventeen inches a year—about half of that in the form of winter snow— capturing an adequate water supply was the key to agricultural success. Valley sites close to water sources were the first, and ultimately the best, farms and ranches in the county. Because the Smiths on their Uncompaghre River homestead and the Shepherds on their ranch off Cow Creek were among the very first to appropriate water, they had senior priority water rights that guaranteed them not only a specified amount of water but the equally important assurance that they would receive all their water before other, junior users—those who had appropriated at a later date. It was the application of the "first in time, first in right" principle. In other words, an 1879 water right, such as the Smith Ranch owned, was (and is) senior to a right filed in 1896 (such as the water right I purchased with my ranch off Dallas Creek), regardless of the amount of water used (limited, of course, to the amount specified in the decree), its location (adjacent to, upstream, or downstream), or the distance from the water source. In the event of a water shortage due to drought, the senior users got first crack at the available river water. Junior users could use their water rights only after the senior users' priority was satisfied.

Water rights served from the very beginning of Anglo settlement as the measure of a land's value. As more and more settlers obtained rights for a finite amount of available water, it became a resource of increasing importance. The water source itself was and is a function of the amount of snow that falls in the San Juans the previous winter. The massive snowfields of the San Juans, in some places measuring forty to fifty feet in depth, are the summer reservoirs that supply the rivers and, eventually, the irrigation canals and ditches. A dry winter means a shortage of summer irrigation water and the likelihood of a poor crop;

but a heavy winter snowfall, combined with cool summer nights and no evaporating winds, can mean adequate water throughout the summer months, if there is a system of irrigation ditches to transport the water to the fields.

Where water is the lifeblood of agriculture, the irrigation canals and ditches are the arteries and veins that transport it. To build the ditches and maintain them, many of the early homesteaders formed ditch companies—one of the first, and certainly one of the most important, cooperative ventures for the pioneers in Ouray County. One owned shares in a ditch company in proportion to the amount of water one had appropriated. If the ditch was designed to carry thirty-three cubic feet of water per second to five different ranches, and one ranch owned eleven feet of the total, that particular ranch was responsible for one-third of the ditch's construction and maintenance costs.

Ditch company members devoted their own labor, tools, and horses to building the ditch, including the headgates where the water was diverted from the river and the necessary flumes to carry the water across deep ravines. They broke boulders with sledgehammers and picked rock walls apart with hand tools or dynamited them; teams of horses pulling slip buckets (sometimes called fresnoes) served as the functional equivalent of today's bulldozers and backhoes to dig and move the shale and dirt within the ditch path. Where the ditch hugged a steep hillside, timbers reinforced the outer wall and plank floors protected the bottom against erosion.

Ditches carried water from a river or creek to as many as ten farms or ranches over distances sometimes greater than ten miles. Sited by eye or with primitive surveying equipment, the ditches usually dropped a foot in elevation for every hundred feet in length. They cut around and sometimes through hillsides and were designed to be deep and wide enough to carry the approved amount of water to the farms and ranches they served. In areas where the country was rough or rocky and the ditch had to wind around a small mountain or large hillside before reaching its final destination, the waterways sometimes took years to build. One eight-mile ditch built in the Cow Creek region of Ridgway in the late nineteenth century took five years to complete. After its builders finally finished constructing a tunnel through a large shale hill, they proudly turned in some water at the headgate. The next day, the tunnel collapsed and the entire hillside slid away, taking with it a one-hundred-foot section of the new waterway; the ditch could not be repaired and was never used again. The local ranchers of the Alkali Ditch Company then spent three more years building another ditch, this one successful, following a different route.

Every day during the irrigation season, a "ditch rider" ensured the proper inflow at the headgate, made minor repairs to the ditch, and kept it free of trash (brush and leaves) so that the water flowed uninterrupted throughout the summer. The county water commissioner today continues the historic practice of ensuring that no ditch takes more water than its legally approved appropriation and that senior water rights take precedence over junior ones. If a ditch is taking more water than its allotment, the water commissioner warns the ditch company to take only its proper amount, and no more. If the ditch company fails to follow the order, the water commissioner can lock the ditch company's headgate. A rancher learns quickly never to anger a water commissioner!

Anyone with a keen eye can trace the path of a ditch by following its high, rounded shoulders as it gently circles around the edge of a hillside before crossing a sagebrush field. Imperial cottonwoods, standing like gigantic green exclamation points against a deep blue sky, guard the ditch banks from the flowing water. A wooden headgate at the first ranch on the ditch path takes in its allotted amount of water, and the ditch continues to circle around the country, a glimmering silver thread in the landscape, dropping in elevation only enough to keep the water moving gently and evenly to the next headgates it serves.

As the number of farms and ranches in the Uncompaghre watershed increased in the early 1900s, particularly down the valley in Montrose, water users in the region lobbied the federal government to build an eight-mile tunnel to carry water from the Gunnison River to the Uncompaghre Valley. The water tunnel was the first major project of the new Bureau of Reclamation, and President William Howard Taft came to Montrose in September 1909 for the opening ceremony. Farmers and ranchers throughout the region turned out for the important occasion, and the Montrose newspaper noted that the 320-pound president, although "not blessed with the athletic tastes which characterized our former president [Teddy Roosevelt], ... ambled the half mile ... round trip without appreciable fatigue."

The intricate system of irrigation canals and ditches constructed throughout the Uncompaghre Valley in both Ouray and Montrose Counties allowed beef and hay production to become an important part of the valley's economy. With connecting rail service over the mountains to Denver and Kansas City available, local pioneer ranchers had the opportunity to supply cattle for regional and national markets as well. Ranchers accustomed to dealing only with local buyers had to learn how the new markets worked, including the transportation requirements for accessing them, as well as the practices of a bewildering array of middleman.

The valley ranches never reached the size of the larger operations beginning to form at the lower elevations in Texas, New Mexico, eastern Colorado, Wyoming, Kansas, and Nebraska. The Ouray County ranches were always relatively small by comparison in both acreage and livestock numbers. In 1910, the average Ouray County ranch was less than four hundred acres and had no more than one hundred head of cattle. The mountainous terrain, high altitude, and short growing season limited the size of ranches far more than the difficulties of obtaining operating capital or credit did. It was hard to raise cattle on land that, in the words of one flatlander who moved to the area, "looks all busted up and stands on end."

Success in the new land had many ingredients. Good health was critical, but so too were water, a prime piece of level ground, a healthy set of reliable horses, and a little luck. Because horses provided a ranch with its only source of transportation and power, the owner constantly kept an eye out for a team of young Belgians or Morgans with the strength to pull a heavy wagon, rock sled, or fresno. He also watched for a young quarter horse that, with patient work, might become a skilled stock horse. A rancher bought or traded for a horse based on its condition (flesh, feet, stamina), conformation (size and muscle pattern), age, intelligence, and skills. If the horse was young, the prospective owner imagined what critical skills it could be trained to perform. An experienced horseman could break a horse for either a saddle or harness, and a well-trained horse recognized what it was expected to do by the sound of a familiar voice, the rein pressure on the bit, and the rider's weight distribution or leg pressure on its flank. A good horseman never abused a horse or broke its confidence by asking it to perform a task beyond its ability.

Horses also helped to identify people. Neighbors and acquaintances recognized a horse or team (and hence the owner) long before they were close enough to greet its owner. Later generations of ranchers have carried forward this equine-owner identification technique and now apply it to tractors and pickups.

Farmers followed a practiced annual routine defined by the seasons. Assuming normal spring weather, the fields had thawed by early April and had dried sufficiently by early May to allow some land leveling, the cleaning of irrigation ditches, and the planting of crops. The previous year's hay supply had to last until new grass sprouted in the spring. One could grow a successful crop if there was nothing wrong with the store-bought seed and if the seedlings were not killed or stunted by a frost after the last day in May. Most important, of course, there had to be a sufficient winter snowfall in the mountains to guarantee an adequate water supply for the summer. If the ditch company that served the farm or ranch needed additional labor to repair winter damage to the ditch, a family member had to perform that task without disrupting the workload of others in the household. A rancher who lost less than 10 percent of his calves to disease brought on by late spring snows had a good spring. Before cattle could be turned out on the summer range, the new calves had to be branded and the cows inspected and doctored for infections or injuries. And as more and more farms and ranches came to dot the land, fences needed to be built, repaired, or replaced with Mr. Glidden's new invention—barbed wire.

A stockman needed ample summer pasture for his cattle and sheep where they could transform high-protein grass into weighty muscle before being sold in the fall. He saved his irrigated meadows to grow grass hay for winter feed and looked to the lush summer grasses of upland meadows at the higher elevations to sustain his herd. Sometimes the stockman homesteaded a quarter or half section for summer pasture. More often, though, he grazed cattle on federal lands administered by the Forest Service and the Land Bureau.

By 1903, the Forest Service, under the direction of Chief Forester Gifford Pinchot, had established a system of grazing permits and fees on the newly established national forests, including the Uncompaghre National Forest. According to local newspaper accounts, the stockmen complained about the new user fee (an "obnoxious tax") and the new forest rangers ("government officers of inferior knowledge"), an attitude carried forward to the present day. Within five years, however, they had reluctantly come to accept the new federal grazing system, although not necessarily the level of the fees or the operating regulations. Local ranchers recognized that the federal government brought peace and rational order to the growing and often violent conflict between cattlemen and sheep men over the use of federal lands. Also, as small operators increasingly conscious of the deterioration of the range, stockmen looked to Washington to protect them from the predatory practices of the larger operators who wanted to monopolize federal grazing lands.

The bread and butter of all county agricultural operations, how-ever, depended far more on the weather than anything else. A successful farm or ranch required a summer growing season of sufficient duration (ninety to a hundred days), mild but not hot temperatures, and timely summer rains. The irrigation ditches needed to flow without interruption from mid-May into late August to compete with the hot winds that could dry out hay meadows and crops faster than water could replenish the weakened plants. A drought (caused by a winter without sufficient snow or a summer without any rain) brought lightning fires and the dreaded grasshoppers. During the late summer harvest season, all the equipment had to be in working order, the horses in good health and flesh, and the weather cooperative (no rain during harvest or early frost) to allow a timely harvest. The rancher prayed that disease would avoid the entire valley during the contagious summer months. If the home garden produced as expected, and mites or fungus took no more than their share, the rest of the family began to can the winter's supply of vegetables, a process that lasted well into the fall.

Once the crops (small grains, hay) were harvested and the calves and lambs had been weaned off the cows and ewes, farmers and ranchers looked for affordable transportation to take their produce to markets offering satisfactory prices. Before 1910, farmers sold their small harvest in the immediate vicinity; only after the construction of trans-mountain railroads did local ranchers ship livestock by rail to regional markets in Denver and Kansas City. The general health of the national economy determined cash prices for almost all the county's agricultural products. A change in the national monetary policy or a drop in the price of silver or gold affected what the mines were willing to pay for oats, bread, hay, pork, eggs, and beef. The local market was generally predictable as long as the mines continued to operate at a profit.

With a good crop and healthy livestock prices, a farmer or rancher would be reimbursed for his labor and be able to bring his bank loan current and purchase the supplies necessary to carry his family through the winter. Ranch and farm families survived the winter by living off the production of the other three seasons. During the winter, they made repairs (to harnesses, clothes, tools, and equipment) and, if the weather cooperated, built new structures. Log houses were expanded—a new bedroom, a root cellar, maybe a wood shed off the side of the kitchen— and livestock corrals and sheds were built or improved. Some trapped beavers or muskrats on the rivers or hunted snowshoe rabbits and turkeys. A buck or doe might appear near the haystacks after a heavy snow, but the early settlers had pretty well decimated the resident deer and elk populations by 1900.

Every winter morning, the rancher harnessed a two- or four-horse team of Belgians, pulled the feed sled up to the haystack to load it with hay, and then drove the team out to the livestock. Other winter chores might include readjusting the large, spiked winter horseshoes; replacing the planks in the box of the spring wagon; or finishing the floor in the bedroom that was started seven years ago. There never seemed to be enough firewood for the cookstove or the fireplace, despite the three cords of aspen and scrub oak cut in the early winter. The rancher used the sawdust generated by the wood cutting to cover and preserve the blocks of ice he cut from a nearby pond and hauled back to the icehouse.

Most important of all for the success and survival of a farm or ranch, everything depended on all family members maintaining their health throughout the year. Every member of the household had a job and responsibilities. A small family could ill afford to have someone struck down by pneumonia or typhoid fever or a broken leg from a horse accident. The division of labor between husband, wife, children, and others in the household was well defined, and each person added to the entire production of the ranch. In case of sickness, or, worse, death, the lost labor had to be replaced by the labor of those who remained. Hired labor was not generally available and was certainly not afford-able for most people. When death did occur, it was closely witnessed and generally accepted as God's will.

The social, religious, and educational lives of all the ranch communities in Ouray County centered on the rural schoolhouses located on the isolated mesas (Log Hill and Hastings Mesa); in the areas of Dallas Creek, Dry Creek, and Pleasant Valley; and down-valley toward Colona. Local farmers and ranchers formed school districts, built one-room schoolhouses, and hired, housed, and paid the teachers. Coal- or wood-burning stoves heated the uninsulated wooden structures, and usually an outhouse and horse shed sat behind the schoolhouse.

A stalled school bus. The burro, recently retired from the mines, refuses to move his passengers in spite of a little help from his friends. Denver Public Library, Western History Collection, #Z-3098

The schoolhouse served multiple functions: it was meeting place, church, dance hall, and education center for children and adults alike. Immigrant parents, sensitive to the growing native-born sentiment against foreigners in the early decades of the century, borrowed grammar and spelling books to improve their English. The school day started at 9:00 A.M. and finished in early afternoon. Some schools, such as the one on Hastings Mesa, operated only in the summer (May–October) because of the heavy winter snows. When a population center shifted to another area in the county, residents attached wheels to the schoolhouse and hauled it off to the new site. The few students who wished to continue on to high school had to travel to Ouray or Ridgway and, if the distance from the farm or ranch was excessive, locate accommodations in town.

At a minimum, farmers and ranchers expected their children to finish the eighth grade; gain a reading, writing, and speaking knowledge of English; and know some American history, geography, and the basic rudiments of mathematics, including the multiplication tables and how to calculate compound interest. A student who continued on to high school in the early 1900s studied algebra and geometry; ancient, medieval, and modern history; botany, geology, geography, zoology, chemistry, and physics; two years of German; English grammar and literature; civics and something called "rhetoricals"; and three years of Latin, including the works of Virgil. Most parents recognized the importance of basic mathematics for their children but failed to see the relevance of Virgil or medieval history for people barely scratching out a living on a subsistence farm or ranch. The skills that guaranteed employment after schooling were learned at home, on the farm or ranch.

Recognizing that their pupils had chores to do both before morning classes and after they returned home late in the afternoon, the teachers seldom assigned homework. Students were expected to study at school. As one early resident put it in a collection of Ridgway reminiscences (*The Way It Was*), "We went to school to learn. ... We didn't learn anything at home." Discipline, when necessary, was administered swiftly and without question by either the parents or the teacher. Punishment usually meant additional schoolwork (such as learning spelling lists or working a set of mathematical problems), although it sometimes took a physical form such as a switch to the back of the hand or buttock.

Success came slowly and incrementally to the county's farmers and ranchers; and it was measured not monetarily but rather to the extent that the family could survive in relative comfort into another season. Because the first homesteaders possessed virtually no savings or safety net, either from the government or from their families, there was a slim margin between surviving into another season and failure. The farmer learned quickly not to abuse the land; he knew its limits in a drought and its possibilities after a rain. In the winter, if hay was in short supply, he sold off cattle to "fit the herd to the [hay] stack." If a farmer could not pay the small county property tax, his place was sold at a sheriff's sale. A debilitating horse accident or serious illness might result in the loss of property. Alcohol took its toll on homesteaders, as did poor judgment such as the initial location of the homestead, the crops planted, or the amount spent on new equipment or an unnecessary luxury.

Not only did many things beyond human control have to go right—the weather, the markets, the family's health—the farmer or rancher and his family also had to manage the limited resources they had at their disposal wisely. Intelligent decisions had to be made in a timely manner: when and for how long to graze a certain pasture; the best time to harvest a crop or wean a set of calves; where and when to market twenty tons of hay and five sides of beef; whom to use as a commission agent in Denver or Kansas City; what to pay for a new baler and how to finance it; the best remedy for water belly in a steer; how, where, and what to pay for a set of good breeding bulls or some young ewes.

The remedies for bad luck, poor judgment, and poor health were few. Like other homesteaders on the dry high plains, farmers and ranchers learned that rain did not follow the plow, nor were prayers for moisture always answered. The government could, and did, change the homestead laws to assist settlers in the arid regions of the country, but Congress could not mandate rain. There were no government services at the turn of the century to advise on irrigation practices, animal health, crop rotation, or planting procedures. An arm lost in a baler could not be reattached or replaced, nor could tick fever, typhoid, or pneumonia be treated effectively by the remedies of the day, which included the application of mustard plasters, matted cobwebs, and leeches, and the ingestion of herbs, castor oil, turpentine, and a wide variety of "snake oils." If a rancher overgrazed a hay meadow in the summer and saved no hay for the winter, he had only himself to blame—and no recourse to an emergency loan from the government. Given the mixture of luck, personal judgment, and limited resources that determined success, it is a wonder that any of the original homesteaders and their families farmed or ranched for as long as a decade, much less for a generation and beyond.

In fact, not many of the original homesteaders remained on their land in Ouray County for that long. A cursory review of county tax records suggests that fewer than one in every five farmers or ranchers who resided in the county in the early 1890s continued to live there in 1910, and only about half of those lived continuously on the same farm or ranch. After proving up their homesteads, many homesteaders sold to neighbors who had the human and capital resources to expand. Some never even proved up; they just departed for destinations unknown, possibly to chase another rainbow farther west, more likely to return to a former home. Quite a few of the ranches were sold to pay taxes and bought by neighbors or other county residents willing to try a hand at ranching. But in a local economy based primarily on the barter system, cash was not readily available, especially to buy land. For creditworthy borrowers, banks extended credit to purchase properties the banks themselves had taken title to after foreclosure. They were less eager, however, to extend loans for properties whose titles they did not hold.

The farms and ranches that endured into the 1920s were far larger than the original late-nineteenth-century homesteads. The average size of a ranch or farm in Ouray County in the 1920s was a little more than four hundred acres. Frame houses had begun to replace the hand-hewn log cabins of the first settlers. Newer and larger barns appeared, as did more diverse outbuildings such as ice and smokehouses, machine sheds, calving and lambing sheds, even bunkhouses for seasonal help. Irrigation canals were enlarged to carry more water to new acreage, which was cleared and leveled with more efficient equipment and seeded with a wider variety of cool-climate grasses and small grains. Tractors, mechanical mowers, and balers considerably enhanced the county's agricultural production. The few well-financed large ranches able to afford the new equipment required less labor to operate. In Ouray County, however, capital was scarce and mechanization occurred slowly. A Farmall tractor eased the harsh burden and slow pace of heavy field labor. But the capital costs of mechanization led many farmers and ranchers into heavy debt, a situation that too often caused foreclosure and failure during the Great Depression of the 1930s.

For most Ouray County residents who sought their livelihood on the land, farming and ranching continued to be a marginal enterprise. Hard work did not guarantee a steady and fair return on one's labor, although lack of effort was a certain and immediate path to failure. People learned never to expect more from the land or from livestock than it could produce. They made no division between labor and leisure; if for no other reason, they could ill afford the luxury of leisure. The one day of rest, Sunday, was given over to God, to His service and His teachings. Their strong religious faith included a vision of the world that did not include human comforts or luxuries, but did include considerable pain and anguish. Life was, after all, a test of man's love for God and each other as much as it was an endurance test; almost everyone, and especially the local town preacher, believed that God's benevolence rarely exceeded His requirements for Christian survival. Almost no one had any reason to expect that life would be physically comfortable or even fair, although parents hoped that their hard work would ease the material burdens of their children. If in their fatalism these pioneers expected little for themselves in the present life, they remained forever hopeful about the afterlife. One lived to survive another season, to honor God, and to love one's family. Through their hardship and because of it, the pioneers shared labor and material goods with each other, recognizing that survival depended as much on neighborly cooperation as on hard work. They were the antithesis of the "rugged individualist," that malignant image created by Hollywood and expanded on by politicians and even historians, who should know better.

Where the standards of hard work, neighborliness, and an abiding faith in a superior being still survive among some families in Ouray County today, these qualities spring from the homesteader experience. It is an experience, it should be remembered, that occurred less than a century ago and is very much alive in the memories of the sons and granddaughters of the original settlers. Their stories and experiences, true or exaggerated, are told and retold, and often embellished, so that almost everyone possesses a common frame of reference. The historical memory may be parochial, insular, and even, in part, artificially romantic; but it remains a precious resource that provides community pride and a standard by which to measure the present and the future.

Chapter Three

Tough Times in Rough Country

Some years ago, during a heavy April snowstorm that prolonged an already nasty winter, a rancher friend and I had lunch together at a local café known for its chicken-fried steak. We shared stories of the heavy calf losses we were both experiencing in that unusually severe spring. My friend, a man in his mid-seventies who had grown up around the mines driving pack teams when not working on his family ranch, said he'd not experienced losses like these since the 1930s. When I asked if those were rough winters too, he said to me: "Not really. The storms didn't kill the cattle, they just starved to death. We just didn't have any feed—the cows, me, or my family." We had finished our meal and were leaving when three teenagers pulled up in a well-polished late-model pickup complete with a chrome running board. They were loud in their friendly but carefree attitude, as all teenagers are, and well dressed. Two wore big black cowboy hats with colorful hatbands and the other had on a baseball cap advertising a local ready-mix company. All wore cowboy boots scruffed by ranch work. As they barged through the door, we gave the boys the right-of-way. Once we were outside, my friend stopped, looked at the pickup and then at me, and said: "You know, Pete, if we had a Depression from time to time it sure would improve the gene pool."

———•—•—

Born into a new century, the sons and daughters of the pioneers who had
come to the county in the 1880s grew up in an era of relative prosperity,
only to face in their middle years an economic depression so severe that
it emptied the county of half of its residents. For Ouray County farmers
and ranchers, the years before America's entry into World War I in 1917
were a time of steady economic growth. Ridgway was a small but mod-
erately prosperous town of almost four hundred residents; increased
agricultural production more than made up for the loss of ore traffic on
the railroad. A record number of cattle filled the loading pens adjacent to
the rail yard north of town throughout October and November awaiting
shipment to Denver and Kansas City. With the government's increased
demand for agricultural products—particularly beef, pork, and mutton—the war years proved as prosperous for local ranchers and farmers
as they did for those throughout the nation. The county reached a level
of prosperity not seen since the mining boom of the early 1890s.

The economic prosperity did not necessarily guarantee the entire
community's support for the war. Most county citizens supported the
war effort by purchasing war bonds and savings stamps and donating
clothing for the troops overseas to the Red Cross. Some of the foreign-
born residents of Ridgway, however, who constituted a quarter of the
population, questioned America's military participation in a European
war. German-born Andrew Sneva, an American citizen and one of the
area's best-known ranchers, was hauled before Ridgway's Hundred
Percent American Club and questioned about his loyalty to the United
States. Amos Walther, the Ridgway bank president, came to Sneva's
defense. As reported in the *Ouray County Plaindealer*, Walther said that
Sneva "should long ago have been notified to quit his ridicule of certain
matters and given a chance. He never was pro-German. He contributed

more clothes than all the rest of the town ... to the Red Cross." The newspaper failed to report if Sneva was, like Fred Sclada, another county resident hauled before Ridgway's nativist tribunal, "forced to kneel and kiss the folds of Old Glory." Ethnic and religious tolerance seem to have been lacking in this ethnically diverse town and county.

Even more devastating than the war for Ouray and the surrounding counties was the influenza outbreak of 1918. Across Red Mountain Pass, just south of Ouray, the *Silverton Standard and the Miner* reported on November 2, 1918, that 128 people had died of the flu (52 in ten days). Herman Dalla, a Silverton resident, recalled the epidemic in a collection of reminiscences titled *Mining the Hard Rock*: "The front of our boarding house was a saloon. Hell, I was only six years old but I can remember the wagon coming from the mortuary and them loading my mother's body into the back. I was watching from an upstairs window. Two of my brothers died. That left nine of us kids with no mom and no dad. Mary was the oldest of us and she kind of took over. We had records of who owed money to Mom and the boarding house, but everybody said they'd paid up. It was rough."

Ouray County's single doctor could not handle the scores of men, women, and children stricken with the fever. Local and state health officials quickly converted hotels in Ouray and Ridgway into temporary hospitals and immediately quarantined them. The same officials detained all visitors coming into the county on roads and at rail depots to determine their point of origin. All schools, churches, and theaters were closed, and public gatherings ceased. Doctors and nurses, already in short supply because of the war, were imported.

In Ridgway, the shortage of grave diggers combined with bad winter storms prevented burials at Dallas Park Cemetery; corpses awaited burial in a temporary mortuary in the town's only drug store, which was located in the bank building. Business at the bank, not surprisingly, dropped off. Cedar Hill Cemetery, north of Ouray, had to be expanded to accommodate the many flu victims, who were buried in a segregated area—quarantined in death as they had been during the last days of their lives. The epidemic finally ended in the summer of 1920, but not before it killed far more county residents than did the war in Europe.

The local mining and agricultural economy in the 1920s never matched the strength of the wartime economy. In 1921, three of Ouray's major mines—the Hidden Treasure, the Revenue, and the Camp Bird—closed because of nonproductive ore and a decline in base metal prices. When the mines closed, rail traffic dropped off, and so too did the Rio Grande Southern's profits. The railroad refused to pay interest on its bonds during the 1920s, and after 1928, failed to pay local taxes as well. The town of Ridgway also fell into arrears when it refused to reimburse the Mentone Hotel $1,500 for the expenses the hotel incurred while serving as a hospital during the flu epidemic. By the end of the decade, half the county's mines had either voluntarily closed or been sued in bankruptcy court.

Although for decades the fortunes of county ranchers had closely followed the local mining economy, after World War I, the prices for beef and lamb were increasingly determined by national and international markets. With Europe devastated and unable to purchase the record agricultural production of the United States, domestic prices for all agricultural commodities, including livestock, declined. Local beef production hit an all-time high in the early 1920s—the railroad put on extra cattle cars to move the livestock to Denver—but smaller ranches with fewer than fifty head found it increasingly difficult after 1922 to compete in the new economic environment. The larger operators, such as the McClure Ranch in Pleasant Valley, with lower overhead costs that derived from economies of scale, managed to survive and even expanded by purchasing smaller adjoining ranches. The larger ranches and farms also possessed the collateral and credit to purchase new farming equipment (mechanized balers, mowers, seeders, and planters, and gasoline-powered tractors to pull these devices), which further reduced their labor costs.

Ridgway in the mid-1920s boasted a bank, two mercantile stores, two hotels, a grocery store, a couple of restaurants, the Methodist Episcopal Church, a blacksmith and wagon repair shop, two boardinghouses, and a drugstore with a marble soda fountain and licensed druggist. The Field Brothers Hardware Store in Ridgway sold McCormick and Deering harvesting machines, Moline plows, Mandt wagons, "horse furnishings," and, for $860, a four-passenger Chevrolet sedan. Household items, including rugs, carpets, iron beds with springs, molding, sashes, doors, and roofing, were all available on easy credit terms. A local livery barn owner, recognizing that machines might replace animals for transportation, began selling Ford cars and trucks. Few farmers could afford these new mechanized vehicles, and even fewer ranchers thought anything with a motor could replace a good horse.

In the 1920s, to help local ranchers and farmers reach the newer, more profitable markets, the state and county began the expensive process of building new roads and bridges and improving old ones. Even with the improved roads, however, the county remained isolated. The high cost of transportation over the mountains (particularly by rail) to distant markets cut deep into the slim profit margins of local ranchers. Out-of-work miners and agricultural workers displaced by the new mechanization added to the county's growing unemployed population.

In view of the slowdown in the economy and the attendant decline in local tax revenues, town and county officials greeted the prospect of Prohibition with a distinct lack of enthusiasm. Saloons paid well over $10,000 a year in license fees into town and county treasuries. When in 1922 Ouray County voters were polled about their views on Prohibition, the practical thirst of local taxpayers overwhelmed the moral stance of the county's "drys." More than three-fourths of the voters supported either a modification of the Volstead Act to permit the sale and consumption of beer and wine or a total repeal of the law.

The Ouray Women's Club protested to the local authorities about the bootlegging, gambling, and "low moral conditions" in Ouray.

Furthermore, they complained, prostitutes were "attempting to co-mingle and converse with the respectable element." Arrest the bootleggers and keep the prostitutes in their "reservation," the ladies demanded, so as to "purify the local atmosphere." The authorities fined John Faletti, a bootlegger and former saloon keeper, $300 and ordered him to spend ninety days in the county jail after they found him in possession of a barrel of whisky. The sheriff emptied the barrel into the river, and the odor could be smelled for miles, the local paper reported. That the town authorities arrested bootleggers but allowed legal prostitution to continue was evidence more of the town's respect for federal law than its moral selectivity.

Although there is a tendency today to romanticize the Roaring Twenties, those years were a time of intolerance, exhibited in a resurgence of nativism. The Ku Klux Klan, a strong political power in Colorado politics in the 1920s, terrorized and intimidated foreign residents, particularly Roman Catholics. Clad in long, white hooded robes, the Ouray County KKK burned crosses on hillsides in Ridgway, Colona, and Ouray. In full regalia, they entered county schools and, before the frightened children, presented the school authorities with Bibles, oversized American flags, and short lectures on what it meant to be an American. Editorials in the *Ouray County Plaindealer* condeming the KKK for "intolerance, bigotry and superstition" did little to halt either the Klan's invasion of the schools or the cross burnings.

Further evidence of internal conflict in Ridgway was the unusual number of fires that occurred after World War I. Early one morning in May 1920, two homemade bombs completely destroyed one Ridgway building and severely damaged another. Almost every downtown building suffered a fire at some time during the 1920s and 1930s, including the Mentone Hotel in 1935, after it had failed and was sold for taxes. There can be no doubt that the town's many wooden structures were susceptible to the everyday hazards of fire. But the presence of so many devastating fires does suggest the presence of ethnic and/or class conflict within the confines of this small western town.

The town of Ridgway, a rail town from the 1890s until the railroad's closure in the early 1950s. Ranching History of Ouray County of the Ridgway Public Library

Nevertheless, against this backdrop of contentious intolerance community events and institutions continued to exist and, in some instances, thrive. Increasing memberships gave the Ridgway Community Church and the Ouray Cattlemen's Association financial stability. Dances at the Sherbino Theater in Ridgway, the Wright Opera House and the Beaumont Hotel in Ouray, and the rural schoolhouses brought friends and neighbors together on Saturday nights. Out in the Cow Creek area, local ranchers built a community hall with borrowed money and paid for it by charging a small entrance fee to weekly dances. The young women in the area raised additional funds by organizing box socials at which beribboned dinner boxes (unidentified as to owner) were auctioned off to the young men in attendance, each of whom hoped to bid successfully for the box assembled by his girlfriend. Ouray's two movie theaters competed for customers, who chose between Mary Pickford in *Tess of the Storm County* and William Farnum in *Riders of the Purple Sage*. The piano player moved between the two theaters with a repertory appropriate for each of the silent movies.

A local promoter brought a mule skinner named Andy Mallory to Ridgway from nearby Telluride and matched him against Gilpin Red, the fisticuff champion of the Leadville mining region. Andy destroyed his opponent before a packed house and soon thereafter was matched against another young Telluride miner, locally known as "Blackie the Kid." Because the local theater could not accommodate the expected crowd, the promoters moved the venue for this Fourth of July holiday matchup to the larger town of Montrose. Two Ridgway locals, one whose promotional skills had been well developed on the area's horse tracks and the other a freighter, served as the referee and timekeeper, respectively, for the scheduled twenty-round match. An arm-weary and badly bruised Andy Mallory threw in the towel in the nineteenth round in what was considered a big upset and a major disappointment to the large betting crowd. The winner, Blackie the Kid, went on to bigger payoffs before larger crowds across the nation as Jack Dempsey, "the Manassas (Colorado) Mauler."

———•·•———

The first to suffer when the Depression came to Ouray County in 1929 was the mining industry. By the end of 1931, more than half the mines remaining in the county had closed. Almost immediately after that the railroad went into receivership and the bank in Ridgway failed, carrying with it the deposits and savings of many local residents. One former resident of the mountain mining district remembers seeing a lone man feeding a sluice box next to a boardinghouse where hundreds once lived. Close by, a father and son were running a tiny gasoline-powered placer machine close up against an old slag heap.

Before federal relief became available, the American Legion and Elks Club organized events to raise money for food relief. Many homes in Ouray and Ridgway were seized for nonpayment of taxes and became county property. Some land seized at that time remains in county ownership today. On a meager budget, the county operated a small "poor farm" where a hired couple fed and cared for ten or so destitute men, mostly old miners who suffered from silicosis. Food barrels in Ridgway and Ouray assisted the growing number of unemployed. Committees solicited additional donations of clothing and firewood. By the summer of 1933, 152 families in Ouray had sought assistance from the local relief committee.

Assistance rendered by the federal and state governments began to arrive in 1934. Public works projects in Ouray repaved and widened city streets, covered the town's sewers, and improved the school playground. In the county, projects funded by the Civil Works Administration (CWA) riprapped the river for better flood protection, built bridges, and regraded and resurfaced roads. Laborers received anywhere from 40 cents to a dollar an hour depending on their skills. A county Civilian Conservation Corps (CCC) camp hired local boys to assist with reforestation and soil conservation projects, including the rechanneling of the Uncompaghre River in Ouray and the expansion of the ball field near the town's hot-springs pool. In the northern end of the county west of Colona, CCC workers converted an old trail to an automobile road, cutting sixteen miles off the trip from Montrose to Telluride. In 1937, Ridgway and Ouray received government funds to assist with the construction of new school buildings.

Already accustomed to hard times and a marginal existence, the local ranchers met the Depression with resignation rather than surprise or shock. Demand for beef, mutton, horses, and hay disappeared as the local mining economy and the national urban economy felt the full effects of work stoppages and unemployment. The major problem facing local ranchers was how to generate cash for the next mortgage payment. Those who managed to transport their livestock to a cash market found that fat steers brought $20 a head at most, and even at that price there were few buyers. A severe three-year drought in the mid-1930s diminished grazing in the valley meadows and mountain pastures. David Lavender, a ranch hand in neighboring San Miguel County, observed in his classic autobiography, *One Man's West*: "I saw the land grazed to dust." No one could afford to purchase the little feed that existed. Livestock were fed as best one could or bartered in exchange for hardware, coffee, flour, sugar, and other necessary household items.

In the county's isolated high mesas and valleys, ranchers fell back on their own resources, making do with their small herds of livestock and vegetable gardens. The Collins family on Hastings Mesa owned a few milk cows and survived on the small cash payments they received ($1.50 per gallon) for the fresh cream they sent on the twice-weekly train to the Ridgway Creamery. With the cash, they purchased flour, beans, and sugar. A neighbor survived by eating jackrabbits and grouse and selling potatoes, turnips, and hay to local freighters. Other residents cut firewood, slopped pigs, ran a sawmill, made small repairs on equipment, and traded sides of beef in Telluride for groceries. When possible, they supplemented their ranch income with odd jobs—they hauled coal and firewood, sold ice, cut ties for the railroad, and hired out by the day on a county crew or neighboring ranch. Years later, Esther Lewis admitted to me, "Sure, they were hard times ... cows, horses and hay ... that's all we had, and all we needed. Neighbors helped each other; we never went hungry and never were cold." But as Esther, who survived the Depression on a Ridgway ranch, reminded me recently: "You have to remember there were limits to neighboring. They had their own problems too."

Almost all farmers and ranchers had to convince their creditors to accept the interest payment on their loan and let the annual principal payment wait another year. Those who tried to lease out a quarter-section (160-acre) parcel of grass could not find takers at $35 a year or even 25 cents an acre. Hay went begging at $15 a ton at the mines, and few people anywhere had the cash for a good saddle horse or a well-broke team. The government made available crop loans up to $300, but mostly for grains (wheat and corn) not grown in the county's cold climate. Ranchers reluctantly sold cows to the government for $10 a head and then sadly watched as they were shot and buried in a huge disposal pit outside Ridgway. Although the government's program to purchase livestock throughout the West decreased cattle numbers, it did little to ease the financial burden most ranchers carried.

With prices for their beef and lamb declining, local stockmen who ran their livestock during the summer on government lands administered by the Forest Service and the Grazing Service could not afford the federal grazing fees. The days of the open range of the late nineteenth and early twentieth centuries, when local stockmen could graze unlimited numbers of livestock on lands loosely administered by the General Land Office and arrange (or fight) among themselves as to who and what (cattle or sheep) would graze where and for how long, had long since passed. In 1903, in response to the overgrazing of public lands, the Forest Service had instituted a permit and fee system for livestock that grazed on public forest lands. A similar system was instituted in 1934, with the passage of the Taylor Grazing Act, on all other public lands not reserved for national parks, forests, or other federal reserves (e.g., wildlife refuges, military reservations, Indian reservations, national monuments, reclamation land). With much of the federal grazing land in the West ruined by the three-year drought in the midst of the Depression, many stockmen gave up their grazing permits even after the government agreed to forgive the modest fees.

Throughout the valleys and mesas, ranch families continued to

assist each other at brandings, ditch cleaning, cattle roundups, thresh-
ing, baling, and the cutting of wood and ice; but each year, the number
of neighbors dwindled. One rancher was found frozen to death in his
cabin; another camouflaged his suicide so his family could collect his
insurance money. After one farmer died of pneumonia, his wife managed, with two young boys, to keep the small homestead together on
the $20 a month she earned as a teacher. Her son Glenn Berry later
wrote in a privately printed family history titled *Hastings Mesa*:
"Mother had no choice but to teach to keep the wrinkles out of our
stomachs." David Lavender remembered one homesteader who strug-
gled to keep his ranch solvent

> with a series of labors no mere animal would ever have
> endured. Lacking fodder one winter, he tore up his mat-
> tress and fed the straw filling to the milk cow. Lacking
> shoes, he wrapped his feet in gunny sacks when he went
> into the snow to work. Starving, he secretly killed and
> butchered his burro, bringing the meat home with glad
> tidings that he had shot a deer. The children never guessed
> the truth; the knowledge that they were eating their pet
> donkey would have caused sorrow and humiliation, and
> they still believe that old Jack wandered off during a
> storm and died.

For everyone, the Depression killed whatever remnant of innocent
optimism survived from earlier homesteading days. In addition, the
Depression had the effect of leveling a local county population that had
only recently begun to delineate itself by wealth. Those who operated and
owned large ranches had to absorb new debts if they wished to remain
in the cattle business. The vast majority of county residents—small
landowners or laborers with only meager resources—either devised new
survival strategies if they wanted to remain in the country or moved on.

Those who chose to abandon their homesteads returned to places they called home in distant towns or cities and moved in with relatives. A few found supplemental employment on the road crews being assembled with federal relief funds. "It helped getting a position," one rancher remembered, "if you were a veteran." One cowboy felt himself fortunate to receive from a local resident a new set of reins, a used bit, and a bag of sugar in return for breaking a horse. Ranch women sold jars of chokecherry and blackberry jam and whatever surplus they could scrounge from their small vegetable gardens. Two ranchers saved their meager grain crop and reactivated their old stills, dormant since Prohibition, then peddled their potent home brew to discreet local customers. A number of hired men agreed to stay on cattle and sheep outfits without wages, recognizing that a single room and two meals a day was probably more than they could expect to find someplace else down the road.

A few ranchers with cash bought out adjoining ranches, admitting their discomfort at taking advantage of a neighbor's misfortune. More common were those who patiently waited for a ranch to fail and then bought it for the amount owed in taxes a year later. Vacant "places" carrying the names of the original settlers dotted the countryside as banks and insurance companies became reluctant owners of enterprises that they could neither sell, lease, nor operate. The dry-land farmers, the last to come into the county and the inhabitants of the worst land, were the first to fail and depart. One abandoned homestead bore a sign that read: "HOMESEEKERS BEWARE. IT'S WATER YOU WANT—NOT HOT AIR."

The isolation and hard work took its toll on homesteaders, particularly the children. Lavender, in his autobiography, remembered with sadness the harsh lives of his neighbors.

> The mental vacuum in which children grew up is incredible. To be sure, there was a one-room schoolhouse nearby (whose short sessions were held in summer, since winter snow made travel impossible), but few of the scholars finished

its six grades, for their services were needed at home. And right at home they stayed, their little bodies bent and hardened under adult labor—and occasional adult abuse—of the cruelest sort. They reached maturity without entering a church or sitting down before a white tablecloth. They never flushed a toilet or saw a railroad or stepped on a cement sidewalk. Their only contact with the simplest "necessities" of modern living came through the pages of the "WISH BOOK"—the mail-order catalog—and they rarely bought what they saw; they only dreamed.

The damage caused by the Depression was as much mental as physical. Men hanged themselves from barn rafters so that their families could collect small insurance benefits, believing they were worth more to their loved ones dead than alive. Ranchers felt trapped by the daily grind of having to care for and maintain their livestock, recognizing that a market economy they knew little about, and over which they had no control, determined their worth. The elderly felt too old to start over and too poor to move, and almost no one possessed skills salable in a depressed national economy. Children hesitated to leave their parents for fear of making a bad situation worse. Everyone had exhausted themselves attempting to replace capital with labor. In the end, for those marginal farmers who failed to make a go of it on a couple of quarter sections, the choice remained bleak—either leave or starve.

By 1940, after the involuntary departure of hundreds of dry-land farmers and ranchers, all that remained of many homesteads were a couple of shade trees around the rock foundation of a sixteen-by-twenty-four-foot house—the wood long ago hauled away for lumber or firewood—and maybe a stone chimney, some cedar fenceposts wrapped with old wire, a rhubarb patch, and a well. If the abandoned house remained, like the clapboard one I found on my ranch, livestock had broken into it and made it a shelter from winter storms. Old newspapers

announcing the next meeting of the local Uncompaghre Darn and Patch
Club and the proceedings of the new Ouray Cattlemen's Association
insulated the interior walls; the second-story sleeping quarters served as
a home for generations of swallows. Flat foundation stones marked the
outline of a small shed; and some rotted posts defined the outer limits
of a fenced front yard where no doubt a vegetable garden once competed with early September frosts.

The surviving livestock operations absorbed the dry-land homesteads
into their grazing operations. The squatters, as the ranchers called the
dry-land farmers, and their "damned fences" had departed for greener
pastures or other occupations in distant valleys and cities. For those
who survived the Depression, the skeletons of these homesteads served
as a visual reminder of how bad luck combined with poor judgment
could devastate the life savings and dreams of an entire generation.

Denver filled with the debris of the great homesteading and farming diaspora. The migration started slowly in the 1920s and picked up
momentum in the 1930s. The forced rural-to-urban exodus was not a
new phenomenon. For centuries, farmers and workers in Europe, New
England, the American South, and Latin America have sought refuge in
cities after experiencing major economic disruptions in the rural economy. Machines displaced human labor in large cotton fields in Georgia
as well as on small hay fields in Ouray County. As Thomas Hardy
expressed it in *Tess of the d'Urbervilles* many years before the Great
Depression, when landowning farmers are forced off the land and the
rural communities lose the people who are the depositories of village
traditions, "the process, humorously designated by statisticians as the
'tendency of the rural population towards the larger towns' [is] really
the tendency of water to flow uphill when forced by machinery."

Finally, through the efforts of the Roosevelt administration, the
national farm economy began to recover in the late 1930s. With the railroad reopened, the Ouray County grain and livestock producers who could
afford the rail shipping rates once again found buyers at their traditional

markets. In 1938, more than 1,400 railcars of livestock (plus an equal number of cars loaded with lumber, ore, and beans) were shipped through Ridgway. Transportation by truck from the Western Slope to eastern markets, although less expensive, was less reliable, too. Until 1939, a paved all-weather road kept open through the winter months from eastern Colorado to the Western Slope did not exist. That same year, the county assessor reported "conditions promising" on farms and ranches with people "planning expansion and improvements. ... It has been a long time since Ouray County has been in a more promising state of well-being."

By the advent of Word War II, the county had transformed itself and settled into two ranching communities, one centered on Ridgway and the other on Colona. Mining continued to be important to the county's economic vitality, but the industry had begun to move on to richer claims in more accessible locations in the United States and cheaper labor markets overseas.

The families that remained in the county emerged from the Depression years with new survival skills that they would find useful in the future. Those who survived the 1920s and 1930s with their land and livestock intact once again reminded themselves (and their children) of life's harsh lessons: avoid unnecessary risks, especially debt; work hard, pray for God's grace, and hope for a dividend of luck; cooperate with your neighbors in good times and bad, especially bad; and remember the adage: Make hay while the sun shines for tomorrow may bring rain. Imbued with a new, grimmer view of life's possibilities, no one expected to be cut any slack, now or in the future. And if they felt like passive agents in a national economic system they neither understood nor profited from, they had at least survived, with each other's assistance. The Depression had created within them a deep suspicion of the city, which came to be viewed as a place where quick-buck operators sucked the productive wealth from the countryside.

Although World War II took away many of the county's young men to Europe and Asia, it also brought a new prosperity to the county's farms, ranches, and mines, if only temporarily. As in World War I, government contracts increased the demand for and raised the prices of local beef, mutton, and base metals. Ranches began to specialize in production practices. Livestock operators no longer attempted to raise both sheep and cattle, nor did they attempt to grow small grains on marginal soils in the cold and semiarid climate; the land could more profitably be used for grazing.

———•••———

By mid-century, the surviving sons and daughters of the pioneer generation had organized their agricultural endeavors so that they could produce more products for distant markets with less labor on larger ranches. Between 1935 and 1950, the county lost almost a hundred farmers and ranchers, their land absorbed by neighbors into production units half again larger than those of fifteen years earlier. New and distant customers, soon to be called "consumers," now wanted their beef "grain fed," which required new feeding practices and more capital. With the improvement in highways, large cattle trucks replaced railcars as the preferred mode of transportation to distant feedlots. The Rio Grande Southern railroad closed for good in the early 1950s when it lost its last remaining mail contracts. Only a short section of rail between Ridgway and Montrose remained in operation to haul out the ore concentrate trucked to Ridgway from the Camp Bird mine above Ouray.

At about the time the railroad announced its closure and the immediate sale of its assets, the Bureau of Reclamation began to study the feasibility of a series of three storage reservoirs, one of which would flood the entire town. Combined with the demise of the railroad, the prospect of a flooded town convinced local shopkeepers and residents of Ridgway's bleak future. Between 1950 and 1970, the town lost about a third of its population. By the early 1970s, Ridgway had barely two hundred people, half its 1920 population. Along with other small towns and villages in rural western Colorado, Ridgway and Colona stood at the bottom of an urban-town hierarchy with Denver at the top, followed in descending order by Grand Junction and Montrose.

Ranching, primarily cattle but also some sheep, and the two major operating mines (Camp Bird and Idarado) continued to give life to the county. A new generation practiced the skills learned from the first generation of farmers and ranchers. And as always, the seasons determined and defined the work associated with the raising of livestock.

Chapter Four

The Seasons of Ranching

When we moved to Ridgway in the spring of 1974, there was little there to attract new residents. The overproduction of beef had depressed cattle prices, a normal occurrence for the livestock market about every seventh year, so ranching was not a prosperous business just then. Most of the older buildings in Ridgway stood empty or had collapsed. On a vacant lot just up the street from the former site of the Mentone Hotel sat Hinchman's Trailer Court, an imperial name for a scruffy collection of rusting mobile homes that possessed all the architectural charm of old railcars. Sitting on concrete blocks without skirts, unable to hide the old car batteries and plastic garbage bags strewn beneath them, the trailers looked as if they'd been arranged by a tornado. On the fence was posted a warning to all who might dare to trespass into this wild kingdom: "Beware of Dog." One assumed the ferocious canines that guarded the eight mobile homes were fed every day, but one was never certain.

Down Sherman Street, the shell of the abandoned Field Brothers Hardware Store leaned on wooden braces; next door, a brick pile marked the site of Otto Mears's elegant railroad building, built in the 1890s, abandoned in the 1960s, collapsed in 1971. Two other abandoned lots served as reminders to the dying town of a massive explosion that ripped through Ridgway in the late 1950s. Dynamite stored in an old building ignited early one morning, killing four townspeople and demolishing much of the old town center. The blast occurred at about the same time the Bureau of Reclamation announced its plans for a series of dams and reservoirs in the Ridgway area. When the project was completed, the bureau said, some valley ranches along Cow Creek and Dallas Creek would be flooded, and a major dam would back waters into the beautiful Uncompaghre Valley and inundate the entire town of Ridgway.

For the next fifteen years, local newspapers offered constant reminders that Ridgway and much of the surrounding area might soon be under water. When Congressman Wayne Aspinall, the powerful chairman of the House Interior Committee, came to Ouray County in 1968, he spoke to a population already resigned to relocation. Aspinall, a longtime advocate of the building of dams and reservoirs throughout the West, told a large and angry audience:

> I know what's bothering Ridgway; it would bother me too if I had something hanging over me like this [reclamation project]. ... If I were a property owner in Ridgway I wouldn't want to put money into a business or improvements as long as there was a possibility there wasn't going to be any Ridgway six, ten or twelve years from now. I also know how some of the ranchers feel. They don't like to see their land taken away from them. Especially in these times of adversity for livestock people and ranchers, we don't like to see this.

With the prospect of seeing what remained of their town and the surrounding valleys become a playground for fishermen and waterskiers, townspeople closed their businesses and moved elsewhere. A few shops remained to serve the diminished and dispirited town, which now had fewer than two hundred residents. "For Sale" signs on every block advertised a bleak future, buildings fell into disrepair, and real estate values plummeted. The Town Council no longer met because no one thought it important to elect one—or a mayor. Yet elected county officials continued to lobby government officials for Ridgway's survival.

To the surprise of almost everyone, in 1971, the Bureau of Reclamation announced the cancellation of the three-dam project. Only one dam would be built, for a thousand-acre reservoir four miles north of town whose waters would not flood Ridgway. Almost immediately the town took on new spirit. In 1972, a school bond issued passed. The year we moved to our ranch on Dallas Creek, the new school had opened, as had a new variety store, and the town had a new sewer system. Soon thereafter, under the leadership of the Jossi family, Ridgway Community Pride raised money and volunteer labor to spruce up the town park and the county fairgrounds at the edge of town.

In the mid-1970s, it was still rare for an outsider to move into Ridgway or to take up permanent residence in the county. A few hippies, remnants of the late 1960s, scratched out a marginal living on the area's small and infrequent construction jobs. The tourists who visited the county to hike or hunt in the nearby mountains stayed in one of the eight motels in Ouray. Some stayed all summer to enjoy the town's cool climate and Victorian charm; most, however, passed through on their way to the well-known vacation destinations south and west of the county—the Grand Canyon, Canyonlands, Zion, and Mesa Verde National Parks. Little disturbed or interrupted the seasonal rhythms of raising livestock, the primary livelihood for the second- and third-generation ranchers who lived and worked in the county. As in the past, some ranchers supplemented their income with other jobs, including working in the county's two operating mines, the Idarado and the Camp Bird.

Few new ranchers had moved into the area since the early 1900s. The three who bought local cattle operations in the 1960s were called "summer people" by the natives. When Deedee and I arrived, our neighbors looked on us with quizzical suspicion. Why, they seemed to be thinking, would *anyone* want to buy *that* ranch in this terrible cattle market? We occupied an unknown space somewhere between the summer people and the natives on six hundred acres of a hardscrabble ranch that had received little care or attention for twenty years.

Starting that spring and for the next decade, before many of them passed away, I came to know many of the sons and daughters of the county's original Anglo settlers—the seasonal patterns of their work and something of the values that governed their lives. Conservative, like rural people everywhere, they suspended final judgment of me and my family until they could determine our tolerance for hard work in this beautiful but tough country. It was spring when we arrived, the season of birth and rebirth.

Spring, I learned, does not come instantaneously in the San Juan Mountains. It emerges gradually, almost reluctantly, in early April, as if God wanted to test a person's patience with snow and cold winds. One day may be warm with a giant snowmelt and the rivers bulging with muddy brown runoff; two days later a damp, chill wind may bring eight inches of wet snow and a cold spell that lasts a week. And all through the spring, the winds blow incessantly, with a monotonous power and velocity that sometimes tears wires from power poles and roofs from barns.

It is during this season of teasing warmth and humid chills that calving begins—the process of birth that gives life to all livestock operations. For everyone on the ranch, it is a season of interrupted sleep; long, cold nights in the calving shed; and many hours on horseback checking, doctoring, and feeding newborn calves. My neighbor, Denise Adams, reminded me not long ago that "if you want to be humbled real bad, then just work around Mother Nature for a while." That first year

I learned that if I didn't like spring on a cattle ranch at 7,200 feet in the heart of the Rockies, then I'd better find a different line of work.

Cows, unlike sheep, are intelligent animals, although sometimes slow to demonstrate it. If raised in the area where they were born, they know from experience where to seek protection from spring storms. Mature cows can calve unassisted in the shelter and isolation of a deep arroyo or beneath a full-grown piñon tree. The first-calf heifers (two-year-olds), which, like teenagers, have not yet reached their full size and development, are a different matter. On our ranch, we keep them close by in a small pasture with good protection from storms and watch carefully in case they need assistance. A large calf may have difficulty passing through the heifer's birth canal. Or the calf may be in a breach position (head back) or upside down. In addition, the young heifer may lack the muscle strength or perseverance of an older cow to push the calf to full delivery.

If after the water breaks and two hours of labor the calf is not forthcoming, we bring the heifer to a stanchion and secure her, and reach a hand (covered by a plastic glove) into her uterus to feel for the calf's two front legs and head. When we locate the legs, we wrap a small chain (similar to a dog's collar chain) around both front legs and attach it to a calf puller, a small ratchet-type winch that performs like a come-along. With careful coordination between the heifer's pushing and the calf puller's gentle pulls, the calf appears—first the front feet, then the head and shoulders, and finally the torso, hips, and hind legs. During the delivery, the midwife must be careful to prevent the laboring heifer from falling on the newborn calf; the choreography between bovine and human must be quick and precise, particularly if the calf is a breach delivery. If the calf is not pulled or is pulled too late, its lungs will fill with fluid and it will drown.

Immediately after delivery, we check to see if the calf is breathing normally. If it is not, we assist it by removing fluids from the mouth and windpipe with a small suction device or administer a small amount of oxygen directly into the lungs. A calf that has been through a tough delivery will be slow to get up even with the urging and nudging of the proud mother. It will lie there taking its first breaths, then slowly and with some difficulty stagger to its feet and instinctively search for its mother's udder. As the mother licks off the afterbirth fluids, the calf finds a teat and hooks on for its first nutritious meal of rich colostrum.

Sometimes a first-calf heifer, especially one that has experienced a difficult and painful birth, will show no interest in her new calf, and in that case we keep the heifer tied to the stanchion so the calf can get its first meal without being kicked or butted away. Usually within a day, however, the heifer and her calf are a devoted pair ready to be turned out of the calving shed and into a small holding pasture nearby with other young mothers and their calves.

Except for the first-calf heifers, most deliveries are routine. If a front leg is curled back to prevent a normal delivery, we reach in, push the unborn calf back into the uterus, and straighten out the leg to allow the cow to deliver without further assistance. If the calf is lying on its back, we can usually turn it gently to prepare it for a normal delivery. Even a breach birth can be accomplished with careful use and positioning of the calf puller.

Sometimes, however, the calf is too big and the cow cannot deliver it, and we must call in a veterinarian to perform a Caesarean section. We have performed them ourselves in an emergency, but doing so exposes the cow and her calf to the risk of internal infection. Most C-sections are routine for a vet, but it takes time and skill to clean the cow and administer a local anesthetic, make the incision and remove the calf through the small cut, and then sew the cow back up through the seven layers of tissue.

In rare instances, the calf dies inside the uterus, a situation that is not always immediately apparent. When this happens, the dead calf may have to be cut into pieces, and each bloated body piece pulled out through the birth canal. It is a bloody, unpleasant task and can make for a long, cold, and sad night. But to successfully assist with bringing into the world a healthy new calf is, for me, the single greatest excitement of ranching. It is a constant reminder that birth is one of God's mightiest miracles.

The new calves are checked every day, because their first six weeks can be difficult ones, particularly when spring storms strike, as they do well into May. Wet snow and mud bring on pneumonia, diphtheria, asthma, and scours—a severe diarrhea that can dehydrate an animal to the point of death. Some calves, weakened by days of cold and wet snows, do not survive and are lost to disease or coyotes. If discovered in time, however, calves with scours or hypothermia can be brought back to a protected shed and doctored with appropriate medicine. All ranchers have on hand, and dispense themselves, various medicines, and all ranchers are well versed in basic veterinary medical techniques. Besides the normal shots of antibiotics, ranchers administer intravenous injections, leg splints, stitches, eye patches, and a wide assortment of pills. We use medicine we know will work in our environment, including a few not designed for bovines. For diphtheria, for example, I have administered Adolph's Meat Tenderizer and Bayer Aspirin with spectacular results. For a particular strain of scours, cattlemen successfully used a hog medicine for years before the USDA banned it. When our own doctoring techniques and skills fail, we call the veterinarian, who drives up from Montrose to give professional (and expensive) assistance.

Throughout the spring calving season ranchers have other responsibilities as well. Fences damaged by drifted snow or elk must be repaired before the summer grazing season. For example, on our two ranches, which together are 1,600 acres, we must inspect and maintain close to nine miles of fence. On our leased summer pastures (6,000 acres), we assist with the inspection and repair of another fifteen miles of fence. Irrigation ditches need to be cleaned of trash accumulated since the previous summer, and the wooden divider boxes in the ditches have to be repaired or replaced. Too often, spring floods tear out irrigation boxes and headgates. As Vaughn Stealey, a neighbor in Cow Creek, once explained to me: "The river has the right-of-way, and she sometimes takes it." When major repairs are required at the ditch company's main headgate, I donate materials and labor to rebuild the structure and its intricate support system of spillways and gravel boxes to ensure a steady supply of water throughout the summer months.

Spring is also the time Deedee and I select and purchase our breeding bulls. We want purebreds as the genetic base for our commercial cattle herd, and for that reason we do not raise our own bulls. At the one or two bull sales we attend each spring, we select four or five yearling bulls to add to our herd, looking for moderate size and the genetic characteristics that promise progeny with good milk and exceptional growth at all life stages. We carefully study the voluminous data provided by the bull breeders so as to select only those bulls we believe can improve our herd's performance and profitability.

The final job of each spring, a rite that reinforces cooperation between ranchers, is branding. We select a Saturday in early May when our branding activities will not conflict with those of our neighbors. If we're lucky, the weather cooperates—no rain and not too hot. I have discovered that the best weather forecaster is the flight service at Walker Field in Grand Junction. One spring day, as ominous rain clouds were beginning to move in from the west, I called the airport and asked the flight service operator about the weather prospects for branding. He responded: "I don't know anything about cattle, but I sure wouldn't want to be flying around Ridgway later this morning." We waited another week for a sunny Saturday.

A visitor attending a branding for the first time is struck immediately by the noise—five hundred cows bawl like muffled foghorns, and their calves, in a separate branding enclosure, return the cries several octaves higher. In addition to the noise, the air is filled with the smell of burnt hair and clouds of dust from horses and riders dragging calves to the branding fire. People scurry about the downed calves with injection guns, ear taggers, branding irons, horn cutters, needles, and knives. Yet for all the apparent confusion, dirt, and pandemonium, branding is a perfectly choreographed cowboy ballet in which everyone moves carefully within a specifically defined space to perform a very specialized job.

There is a definite hierarchy of skills at a branding. Probably the most highly prized job is that of the roper, who must quietly and gently take his or her horse in among a pen of five hundred bawling calves and, without exciting them or stirring them up, lasso the calf's hind legs with a single swing of the rope. It takes a well-trained horse, one accustomed to ropes flying about its head and flank, to keep calm while recognizing which calf its rider wishes to capture and putting the rider close to the selected target. When the horse feels the pressure of the rope dallied (wrapped) on the saddle horn, it moves quickly but gently to the branding fire, dragging the ninety-pound calf behind. Then the work for those on the ground begins.

One of the two wrestlers, the flanker, meets the roped calf; with one hand, he reaches over the calf and grasps its outside front leg, with the other hand, he grabs the loose skin of the calf's flank. In one quick motion, using his knee for leverage, the flanker heaves the calf off its feet and throws it to the ground. He immediately drops one knee down on the calf's neck while holding the calf's front ankle in a hammerlock. In the meantime, the other wrestler has caught one of the calf's hind hoofs and simultaneously pulls back on the leg as he sits on the ground and thrusts the calf's other leg forward with his foot. The calf is immobilized as the rope is cast free from the calf's hind legs. The calf, now stretched out on its flank, is branded with the owner's mark, a two- or three-character (letter or number) brand that is, like a commercial trademark, registered with the state. The hot branding iron is applied quickly and firmly to the calf's flank or hip, the brander being careful not to blotch the mark. The hot irons burn through the hair and into the flesh, leaving a flesh scar that, after it heals in two weeks, can be deciphered by other cattlemen and state brand inspectors. Our brands

(/D/ and DD) are the marks that verify our ownership of our livestock (including horses). When animals change owners, they are rebranded with the mark of the new owner.

In addition to the brand, the calf is given a set of vaccination injections, its horns are cut or burned off with a hot iron, an identifying small triangular cut is placed in the right ear, and, if it is a bull calf, it is castrated. Castration is performed by someone proficient with a small knife who slices off the top of the scrotum and gently squeezes out and removes the two testicles. These are saved for a Rocky Mountain oyster fry the next day. Branding is a stressful experience for the young animal, but within two or three days, it is fully recovered from the physical shock of the hot irons, the castration, and the vaccinations.

Neighbors on the Double D Ranch gather to assist at the spring branding. Courtesy of Peter R. Decker

Depending on the number of calves to be treated, the branding process can last for some hours. On our ranch, we normally work and brand five hundred calves in six hours, assuming clear weather and no injuries. It is tiring work for everyone, and it can also be dangerous; there must be complete coordination among all participants, including horses, so that each knows the location and job function of the other. When there are two branding crews working side by side, it is even more important that everyone know what they are doing. The branding arena, with horses dragging bawling calves, young children and old men carrying hot dehorning and branding irons to and from a portable stove powered by a small propane tank, and twenty people working within the same confined area with knives, needles, tag applicators, and vaccination guns, is not a workplace that meets OSHA regulations. Nor is the work divided by gender or age, except maybe for the wrestlers—strong young men who must, hour after hour, use their strength to overpower and hold down a steady supply of terrified calves and be willing to suffer the cuts and bruises administered to their legs by the struggling animals.

Over the years, I've seen the sharp hoofs of calves slice open the legs of wrestlers, and I've watched other wrestlers cut off their boots because the boots wouldn't slip off over their swollen ankles and feet. One year at our branding, a neighbor vaccinated me (mistakenly, I assumed) for shipping fever. I suffered no ill effects, but neither did I find that I traveled any better that summer. A few times, a crew member has shouted at me: "Damn, Pete, be careful the way you swing that iron. It's one hot son-of-a-bitch." One year at our branding, a young horse carrying John Burkdoll, my foreman, went over backward when a roped calf shot under its belly. Fortunately, John bailed off to the side before the saddle horn implanted itself in his chest. On another occasion, a neighbor's eight-year-old son badly burned his hand when he picked up a hot branding iron; the next year, however, he carried irons back and forth to the fire for five hours without injury, complaint, or relief— and wearing gloves.

The ranch owner places his brand on a small calf while the flankers stretch it out. The calf will also be administered a vaccination and, if male, will be castrated.
Ranching History of Ouray County of the Ridgway Public Library

A branding is as much a social occasion as it is a team sport. It is a time to "neighbor," to visit with friends and relatives who have come to help out. Over a large noontime dinner, the ingredients supplied by the participants and prepared by some of the women in attendance, people exchange local news and gossip, renew friendships, and make plans for the following week's branding at a neighbor's ranch. Branding is a community event, a cooperative effort. The tasks at hand could not possibly be performed without the willing assistance of friends and neighbors. A branding is like many other cooperative ranch efforts (ditch cleaning, haying, the fall roundup): the final outcome is larger than the sum of the individual tasks.

In mid-May, as the grass comes on stronger with each passing day, the cow and her calf adjust to the new, higher-protein diet of sweet young grass, which adds considerably to the volume and nutritive value of the cow's milk and thus to the calf's weight. A mature cow with a calf by her side eats twenty pounds of grass a day. Hay, although nutritious, is never more than a poor substitute to fill the void between late fall and late spring. When the meadows begin to turn green, a cow will turn up her nose at hay and walk miles to chase a few blades of green grass.

By early June, we're ready to load our cow-calf pairs on trucks and take them to their summer meadows. Some ranchers lease their summer meadows from another rancher; others lease United States Forest Service (USFS) lands. Under the provisions of their leases, the USFS specifies the number and type of livestock (yearlings, cow-calf pairs, or sheep) and the grazing period (usually mid-June to early October). In return for the right to lease these remote lands, the rancher must care for the livestock; pay a monthly fee for each cow-calf pair, bull, yearling heifer, or steer; and build and maintain all fences and water holes. These summer permits are valuable assets. They are reasonable in cost, but more important, they allow ranchers to remove their cattle from lower-elevation meadows on their own ground, which are given over to the growing of grass hay for winter feed.

In the high country where we summer our cattle, we spend at least a day a week on horseback inspecting the cattle for foot rot, lump jaw, and respiratory infections, and looking for "dogie" calves without mothers. It is here on the summer range that good cowboy skills are called for—not necessarily the skills associated with rodeos, but the common everyday working skills rarely portrayed in beer commercials or by the Marlboro Man.

Over the years we've had both good cowboys and those of the "big hat, no skills" variety. One who fit the latter description joined us late one spring, bringing with him a string of three intelligent-looking horses. I'm sure he expected that his first job would be accomplished on horseback. Unfortunately for our new hire, however, earlier in the day my foreman had discovered a badly decomposed cow in an irrigation ditch on the north end of the ranch. The cowboy was told the first afternoon of his employment to take the tractor and drag the cow out of the ditch. He returned an hour later and declared: "I didn't sign on this outfit to be draggin' stinking cows out of ditches." I paid him for half a day's work, and he and his three horses moved on down the road. I felt bad that we didn't get to see those horses work.

Skilled cowboys always know where in a three-thousand-acre pasture the cattle will hole up in the heat of the day, and where they can be found at sunset. They can pair up fifty cows and calves in an open meadow and load the same number on a truck without assistance and without injuring or overheating the cattle. They know how to recognize sick cattle; they can rope a three-hundred-pound wild steer in the open or at a fast gallop through the timber, wrestle it to the ground, and with a knee on the steer's throat and a hand pressing against its flank, reach with the free hand into a pocket, take out a needle and syringe, and fill it from a penicillin bottle held in the teeth. The cowboy's horse throughout this doctoring procedure is standing motionless nearby with the rope dallied or tied to the saddle horn, ready to take up the slack in the event the calf suddenly tries to escape. Once the injection has been administered, the cowboy removes the rope from the calf's head and releases it. Rider and horse then continue their hospital rounds looking for other sick animals, always ready to make an assessment of the appropriate medicine with which to doctor the animal.

Good cowboys, and not all of them are males, by any means, are only as good as the horses they ride. They can judge a horse's temperament and athletic ability by watching it move in a corral and determine quickly, on the horse's first encounter with a cow, if it will make a safe and reliable cow horse. Training a good cow horse takes patience, sometimes infinite patience, even if the horse has a quarter horse lineage and displays some "cow sense." Teaching a horse to follow a young calf or an old bull, to cut, to change leads, to feel comfortable with a rope flying all about it, and to remain calm in loud and often dangerous circumstances may take years of patient training; or the horse may instinctively pick up those skills in a year. Then there are horses, like people, who never learn—out of stubbornness, stupidity, or both.

For some ranchers and most cowboys, raising cattle is only an excuse to work on horseback. And working cattle on a well-trained, intelligent, athletic, and calm cow horse is indeed one of life's great pleasures. On the other hand, working cattle with an unwilling partner can be, literally, a super pain in the ass. I'd rather spend five hours in a dentist's chair undergoing root canal work than five minutes in a saddle fighting a stubborn bronc whose mind is on a bucket of grain rather than the work at hand.

Ranch work, even with a good horse, is not always "round 'em up and head 'em out." John Wayne and his hooting and hollering cowboy crew may have moved their critters at a fast gallop, running valuable weight off the cattle, but then again, Hollywood never concerned itself with the economics of cattle raising, only the imagined romance. The romance of the job disappears quickly when you have to ride drag (at the rear) to a bunch of tired bovines, all swarming with flies, on a dusty road in the middle of a hot summer afternoon. Nor do I find it particularly pleasant to work cattle in a blizzard, trying all the while to stay warm and keep my horse from slipping out from under me. Hitting the deck on a slab of ice can break a leg—the rider's, the horse's, or both. And rolling off a cliff with a horse, as I once did, escaping with only a broken leg, is an experience I, and my horse, do not wish to repeat. If the accident were to be repeated, however, I'm certain my horse would, to put me out of my misery, shoot me.

Riding the summer range is the most enjoyable of all ranch tasks, but it is not, alas, the most common one. Deedee and I spend most of our summer hours irrigating the valley hay meadows; irrigation commands our constant attention and labor. It is on the hay meadows that a ranch produces its winter feed, and a good or poor hay crop can make or break a ranch. One cow will consume about two tons of grass hay in the winter, or about the expected production of one acre of well-irrigated valley ground. For this reason we devote considerable time and effort throughout the summer to irrigating our meadows properly. It is backbreaking work, done on foot with shovel in hand, hardly the image of the cowboy riding through the sagebrush whistling "Home on the Range." There is never enough water in our allotment to irrigate all the meadows at one time, so we move the water from one meadow to the next through an intricate system of ditches and laterals.

The water from the main irrigation ditch moves by gravity into a series of lateral (feeder) ditches through wooden headgates, or slide boxes, that regulate the amount of water that enters them. These feeder ditches run along the top edges of all the meadows. When a feeder ditch is full, the irrigator digs a series of cuts in the sod bank to allow water to flow out onto the field. An irrigator with a keen eye and some experience knows how much water to allow out of each cut so as to soak the selected portion of the field in a twenty-four-hour period. If the ranch's water right is of sufficient quantity to allow other laterals and ditches to be utilized simultaneously, the process is repeated at another site. The next day the irrigator checks to see if the water reached the bottom of the meadow. If it did, the cuts are filled with sod and the water is allowed to move down the lateral to a new series of cuts, or into another lateral with another series of cuts. Some small meadows can be irrigated in a day; other larger ones (between fifty and eighty acres) on our ranch can take as long as ten days to irrigate properly.

When the meadow is completely soaked, except for the incorrigible high spots water will not reach (only God irrigates the high spots!), the water flows out of the irrigated field at the slide box and is transferred by gravity down the main ditch to the next headgate in the adjoining meadow and its associated lateral ditches. The topography of our ranch allows us to recapture water that flows over one upper meadow and use it in two additional lower meadows. By the time the water leaves the ranch at the lower end, we've about "got all the wet out of it." Once all the hay meadows have been irrigated, the entire process is repeated—with luck, two or three times between mid-May and mid-August, by which time the hay is ready to cut.

Water, not labor, is the element that distinguishes between a marginal outfit and a successful one. It is easy to determine which ranches have the best (more senior) water rights and which ones must survive on marginal rights, in terms of both seniority and quantity. The most senior water rights in the county are on land around Colona, where the first homesteads, like the Smith Ranch, filed for water in the 1870s and early 1880s.

There is a saying about water that "it is better to have a shovel upstream than a piece of paper downstream"; and while there is pragmatic logic to this observation, and upstream users may from time to time take more than their legal share, most ranchers are careful to abide by the water laws. There are, of course, occasions (particularly in a hot, dry summer) when water thefts occur; and the disputes sometimes turn mean and violent. I once leased an irrigated meadow to a neighbor who had to share water in the same ditch with an ornery character known to me only as Old Man Harris, whose reputation for stealing water was well known. In the early morning hours before sunup, he'd roll rocks in front of my neighbor's headgate. The rocks cut the water flow in half and diverted into Harris's ditch twice his apportioned share. One morning, my neighbor and I caught Old Man Harris at work moving boulders around at the headgate. "See," my neighbor said to me, "that son-of-a-bitch has moved those rocks around so often they're all as round as bowling balls. Hey, Harris," he screamed, "I'll put this shovel right through your God-damned chest next time I see you messin' with my ditch." Once caught, Harris ceased his early morning water raids—until the next year, when the threats had to be repeated.

Another rancher friend of mine believed his neighbor, known for his strong religious views and pious nature, was stealing his water. Early one morning, hidden in a bunch of willows close to the headgate, my friend intoned in a deep, Godlike voice: "Remember one of my commandments, my son: 'Thou shall not steal from thy neighbor.'" Miraculously, my friend's water was never again tampered with.

Timely rains add considerably to the volume of hay, although rains in June or July are rare. Chemical fertilizers also increase the volume of a hay crop. Some years ago, chemical companies convinced ranchers to apply nitrogen and phosphate to their meadows. The chemicals were effective, and the doubled volume of hay made it well worth the cost of buying and applying them. In addition to water and fertilizer, the third variable that determines the volume and quality of hay is the temperature. Late frosts in May or early June can freeze grass already two or three inches high, stunting the final crop; midsummer hailstorms will severely injure the grass; and late-summer frosts will deplete the protein in a plant, reducing its feed value to the animals. Against these natural catastrophes there are no controls or protection. Ranchers hope for warm but not hot summer days, cool but not cold nights, and enough snowpack in the mountains to fill our water needs throughout the short growing season.

Modern equipment has changed some aspects of ranching, but not all. Some of the manual skills associated with ranching—good horsemanship and irrigating—have not changed since the first settlers came into the area. Training a good cow horse, roping a calf and dragging it to a branding fire, and crafting a wooden irrigation box are necessary skills all ranch children for generations have learned at a young age.

Backhoes and bulldozers are far more efficient for building and cleaning ditches than a team of Percherons with a slip bucket, but these machines cost in excess of $50,000, and most ranchers, myself included, lease rather than own them. Ranchers capable of the large capital outlays required to own these machines must incur the additional costs of building storage sheds and machine shops to maintain and repair them.

My largest equipment expense is for haying equipment. A generation ago, mowing, baling, and stacking machines were powered by horse teams or small tractors. Today, high-horsepower self-propelled swathers can cut a sixty-acre hay field in the same amount of time it once took a horse-drawn mowing machine to cut a ten-acre patch. Andy Soderquist, a local rancher in Colona, says he and his wife can go out after supper with his equipment and do in an evening what it took his father and three hired men a day to do with teams of horses.

Large balers pulled by 160-horsepower tractors can bale up to one hundred tons a day, an amount that in the 1920s took a week to package. For the pioneer generation, one hundred tons was an entire summer's crop. Modern self-propelled stack wagons can pick up seventy-five-pound hay bales off the ground and transport them in neat two-ton packages to a storage yard—and in a third of the time it would take a two-man team to do it. Anyone who has had to buck five hundred bales off the ground onto a wagon on a hot summer's day by hand, and then unload and stack them, looks with great envy on someone with a mechanized stack wagon. They may add to the ranch's expenses, but they sure save on the back.

All ranchers in this part of the country stack hay in large enclosures conveniently located on the ranch, sometimes covered but always surrounded with high fences to keep out deer and, especially, elk during the winter months. The hay is stacked in a configuration based on the size and shape of the bales (round, square, or rectangular; each weighing anywhere from sixty-five pounds to one ton). These hay yards will be accessed every day for cattle feed for five months—from about the first week in December until the first week in May.

The process of haying is not in itself complicated, but it can be time-consuming and can extend into early fall, especially when late-summer rains or equipment breakdowns cause delays. Balers require constant care and maintenance. Their gears must be greased, the baling twine replenished hourly, and there are myriad belts, chains, gears, and sprockets to be inspected and adjusted daily. When breakdowns occur, as they always do, the haying operation comes to an abrupt and untimely halt until repairs are made.

Like most ranchers, I keep a small inventory of parts (couplers, filters, belts, chains, etc.) on hand, and these are frequently replaced and updated, but I never seem to have the part I need to get back into operation. Nor is the necessary part (a drive shaft, clutch assembly, or sometimes something as minor as a small spring) available at the implement dealer in Montrose or in Denver, but there is one, I'm informed, in a small town in Iowa. For the cost of a week's groceries, John Deere will happily ship it to me air freight for next-morning delivery. And, of course, in my impatience to get back in the field and take advantage of the good weather, I pay $60 to have a $5.98 spring flown in by Federal Express from Davenport, Iowa. I've also experienced more serious breakdowns (broken clutches or transmissions) when I've had to haul the equipment to the implement dealer in Montrose and lost a week of valuable time during the height of the haying season. All ranchers hope that repairs are minor, the rains are brief, and that all the meadows will be cut and baled by Labor Day.

Finished or not, everyone takes a four-day break from haying over the Labor Day weekend. It is the time of Ridgway's major event, both for its own residents and for the tourists who come to see it: the two-day rodeo and 4-H Club competition. The 4-H competition is an important occasion for the kids in the county, particularly those who live on ranches, who have worked all summer with their animals (hogs, lambs, or cattle) in the hope of winning a blue ribbon in their respective class. Before the show, parents help their sons and daughters fit and trim their animals and get them set up in the show barn, and then they let the kids spend Friday night in the barn with the animals before the next day's competition. It is a tough night for most of the 4-H contestants, for on Saturday the kids will see their lambs and steers auctioned off to the highest bidder and shipped off to the slaughter plant. Despite receiving the sale proceeds

A cowboy at the Labor Day rodeo is transferring his roping skills from the open range to the Ridgway rodeo arena, where two other cowboys attempt to "bulldog" the 800-pound steer. *Ranching History of Ouray County of the Ridgway Public Library*

(and if the animal is the Grand Champion, these can be impressive), it is not easy for a young boy or girl to say good-bye to an animal that, over the course of half a year, has become a member of the family.

For a few years, our ranch hosted an event over the Labor Day weekend pretentiously named "The Double D Ranch Cowboy Polo Tournament." The game can best be described as semiorganized mayhem played, with minimum rules, on horseback. There are four riders to a team, and the object is to hit a beach ball with a straw broom (cut off and taped at the base to give the hitting head some firmness) through opposing players and horses and into a goal at the far end of the arena. The few rules that exist are for the protection of the horses—no tripping or running into the front or side of a horse is allowed.

We usually attracted at least four teams from neighboring ranches.

One year, our team played against the J Bar M Ranch, our neighbors to the east, who mounted a strong team led by a fine horseman, Dale Burkdoll, the brother of my foreman, John. In the middle of the game, just before the intermission, John backhanded his broom into the face of Dale's horse. The horse quickly threw back its head and caught Dale just above the right eye. Dale fell from his horse and lay semiconscious on the ground, a nasty gash on his forehead. We stopped the game to inspect him. John dismounted, went over to the cooler to get a beer, inspected his brother, and announced to the players and spectators, "It's nothing serious, just a small cut below the eyebrow." Dale agreed as he shook himself to full consciousness with the assistance of his brother's beer. Despite the heavy flow of blood from his "cut," he urged us to continue the chukker. At halftime, Dale's mother, who was watching the game from the sidelines, inspected her son and suggested to me and John that Dale should be taken to the hospital in Montrose for some professional attention, or at least a second opinion. "No," John said after another quick inspection of the bloody eyebrow, "it ain't too serious, Mom, he'll be okay."

John was good at all sorts of ranch doctoring. He could sew up a prolapsed cow in a dark barn and had once, in an emergency, performed a Caesarean section to save a cow and her calf, although the cow later died of peritonitis. John enticed Dale into the barn with another beer and said he'd take a couple of quick stitches in the eyebrow and they'd be ready to resume play shortly. We enjoyed some cold beers and let the horses rest, and fifteen minutes later John and Dale emerged from the barn, John wearing the proud smile of a doctor who has successfully completed a life-saving surgical procedure, and Dale with his eye stitched closed. Mrs. Burkdoll looked shocked. "It didn't look that bad to me," she said to John. "I thought maybe just a couple of small stitches and a butterfly bandage." "Oh, no," John the experienced surgeon replied, "it was really big and deep ... needed some major repairs ... large stitches."

We finished the game and won, I think, by a score of 6–4, but only after John blindsided Dale a couple of times in the last critical chukker. After the game, when she saw blood still oozing from the stitched-up eye socket onto Dale's shirt, Mrs. Burkdoll ordered us to take her youngest son to the hospital. When we arrived at the emergency room, the attending physician looked at the stitched eye, then at John and me, and asked: "Who did the stitch work?" "We did," John admitted proudly, as if he'd been part of a famous plastic surgery team. As the doctor began to cut the stitches to open Dale's eye, he said to the two of us, "Well, I guess we'll just have to send you boys back to medical school or take your license away." The next day we played the Sleeping Indian Ranch in the final and lost, but only because they'd brought in a cow-boy with a lot of polo experience. Nor did it help our cause that Dale was the referee.

Win or lose, the Labor Day weekend was never complete without attending the great Sunday night dance at the Cow Creek Community Hall. The fellowship of other ranchers, their stories and laughter, always reminded me why I lived and worked in Ridgway.

* * *

Early fall, with frost in the air and the likelihood of snows at the higher elevation, is the time to bring the cattle down from the high summer pastures to the newly harvested hay meadows. We expect the calves to weigh almost five hundred pounds, a gain of more than four hundred pounds over their birth weight last spring, and the cows, despite their nursing calves, to have maintained their flesh throughout the summer. During the fall roundup, with help from friends and neighbors, we search the entire summer ground (often as much as ten thousand acres), taking days to ride and gather the areas known to be frequented daily by the cattle (open meadows, salt licks, and water holes) and also the less accessible gullies, timbered hillsides, and heavy brush. We gather the cattle from an area within a five-mile radius and trail them into a fenced section (640 acres) of pasture where they await trucking back to our winter quarters.

Inevitably, the number of cows and calves brought to the summer country in June does not match the count in early October. A handful of cows will have died from larkspur poisoning (a flowering plant which, when ingested, causes the blood to thicken), one or two will have been lost to lightning, and another will have died of unknown causes. If we see the carcasses during the course of the summer, the fall tally might match the count after roundup. If not, as is almost always the case, we have to mount up once again to search for the renegade cows. One year, after Deedee, John Burkdoll, and I spent three full days looking for four stray pairs, we finally gave up the search. All eight animals showed up in the middle of winter down on the San Miguel River, almost ten miles from our summer range, a bit thin but nevertheless alive and not particularly happy about being discovered.

When they are returned to the meadows on the main ranch, where there is still some grass remaining after the haying, the cows and calves must adjust to a lusher grass than the feed they left behind in the high country. Once accustomed to the feed, however, the calves continue to gain weight, both from their mother's milk and from the tasty native grasses they are learning to graze.

By early November, the calves are weaned. The cows need the opportunity to rest from their nursing chores and put on weight before winter arrives. The calves too, six to seven months of age now and of sufficient size and maturity to be independent of their mothers, are ready for a life of their own. When their calves are taken from them, the cows bawl throughout the night and search frantically, but the calves have been moved to a distant place (on or off the ranch) where they cannot hear their mothers bellowing, and their mothers cannot hear them. The vaccinations we give the calves for shipping fever, pneumonia, and black leg improve neither their physical comfort nor their mental disposition, but within three or four days they have settled down into a new feeding regime of full-time grass.

Some ranchers, myself included, immediately transport the newly weaned calves on large cattle trucks, each with a capacity to hold one hundred calves, to a nearby auction market, allow them two or three days to recover from the stress of weaning, and sell them. Typically the buyers are feedlot operators who purchase calves in the fall, feed them on a diet of hay and corn for approximately six months, and then sell the steers and heifers at an average weight of 1,150 pounds to one of the major beef-packing companies. Monfort, Excel, and Iowa Beef Packers slaughter the animals and process the carcasses into various cuts (T-bone steaks, rib roasts, flank steaks, etc.) for distribution into retail markets. Sometimes, depending on feed prices, we retain ownership of the calves in the feedlot and sell the finished cattle directly to a packer.

The only calves we do not sell are the heifers we retain as replacements in the cow herd. We spend considerable time selecting them based on their size, conformation, and genetics. In eighteen months, these heifers will deliver their first calves. The cull cows—those that did not breed during the summer, the poor performers who produced small calves, and those showing age (bad teeth, eyes, feet, or udders)—are shipped to the auction market, where they are sold for hamburger meat. I learned the hard way that there is no money to be earned, and much to be lost, by maintaining and feeding a cow that cannot produce a healthy calf each spring or a 450–500 pound calf by weaning time in mid-October. We also sell the older bulls. They seem to lose their aggressive firepower around the age of five.

Fall in western Colorado is a season of transitions, from summer green to winter white, from sleeveless shirts to goose-down jackets. Ducks and geese appear, moving south toward winter feed and cover. It is the time when we most enjoy the beauty of the landscape, a time to relax and recall why we were attracted to the area in the first place. There is time for a horseback ride with Hilary, my daughter, to remind her (and myself) that horses can be used for pleasure and not just work. The horses recognize the distinction, too, and enjoy a leisurely romp across an empty meadow or a stroll along a mountain trail. There's time for a walk up Cow Creek to outsmart a few brookies and rainbows, and maybe a hike into the nearby mountains to witness the explosion of colors brought on by an early fall frost.

We try and ride into the high country before mid-October, when hunters come into the mountains of western Colorado like an invading army. The county is home to a large number of deer and elk (well in excess of 20,000 according to Ken Miller, the local state game warden), and local ranchers are pleased that these herds are "harvested" each year. In cold and heavy snow years, area ranchers lose considerable hay and spring pasture to starving deer and elk.

There is a long tradition of hunting in Ouray County. The pioneers survived in part on wild game, particularly deer and elk. By the 1920s, however, the herds had been decimated. Only with the advent of state hunting laws and the importation of elk from Jackson, Wyoming, in the 1930s did the big game herds regenerate. Today, the large elk and deer population is an attraction to tourists and large numbers of hunters, but a nuisance to ranchers.

I am not a hunter. In my youth, hunting was not, for me, a rite of passage. Also, I spent too much time in Laos and Vietnam camping out in the mud with live ammunition flying around my head to voluntarily experience a similar environment in my own backyard. Today, my hands shake when I hold a rifle. But we do allow a handful of hunters on the ranch. They provide some supplemental income to our ranch and keep the elk and deer populations to a size consistent with the available resources. There are also some townspeople who need the meat, and I much prefer they make use of an elk steak than see a pack of coyotes hunt down an old cow elk too weak to survive another winter. Those hunters looking for the thrill of the kill or a trophy bull whose head they will mount over the wet bar at home are not welcome.

There is still, however, work to be completed before winter. Wood must be cut for supplemental winter heat in the ranch houses and the shop. The oil and filters on the tractors and trucks must be changed in preparation for subzero weather; a temporary patch on an irrigation ditch made in the rush of the summer needs a more permanent repair before spring, as do some boundary and cross fences; I need to work with a young colt to make him more comfortable with a different bit, do some additional work with him crossing streams, and get him accustomed to a rope swinging over his head, around his flanks, and under his belly.

———•—•———

About the time we celebrate Thanksgiving, winter is upon us, a season that will bring an average of seven feet of snow. It is the time of year when we confront nature's full force head-on, and never with adequate protection to keep us and our livestock comfortable. Riding horseback into the fury of a blizzard only to find three dead cows smothered by snow in a deep gully tries my patience with the entire business of ranching. When I think back to a pleasant summer ride in the high country and then contemplate the prospect of a long, cold winter, I sometimes find myself living my life somewhere between Hemingway's youthful dictum "life is a fine thing and worth the living," and Karl Krous's cynical conviction that "life is an effort and deserves a better cause." Winter can turn the most dedicated rancher into a bitter, if not broken, cynic.

By the end of November, snow covers the pastures and the cattle are looking for additional feed. The first priority throughout the winter, regardless of the temperature or depth of the snow, is to feed all the animals. In normal temperatures (zero to twenty-five degrees), we feed each cow a minimum of twenty pounds of hay a day; when temperatures fall below zero, the ration is increased to thirty pounds. We unroll large, round hay bales, approximately eight hundred pounds each, off a bale feeder hooked to the back of a tractor, like unrolling a carpet. A few ranchers feed small bales off the back of a truck or wagon pulled by a pickup or tractor. Some of the old-timers still use a team of horses, believing, rightfully so, that it's easier to move a team than to jump-start a pickup at thirty degrees below zero. We feed our five hundred cows more than a thousand tons of hay through the winter and into the spring.

Severe blizzards cause burdensome problems for man and beast. So as not to interrupt the daily feeding operation, we try to keep all the ranch roads clear of snow. Throughout the winter we watch the livestock for signs of respiratory diseases. Sick animals are rounded up on horseback, brought to the corrals, placed in a squeeze chute, and doctored. To provide adequate water for the stock, we punch and chip holes through the ice daily at three stock ponds and along the creek. And finally, we keep the vehicles in constant repair to ensure their daily operation in subzero temperatures.

Cattle at a feed ground. Enough hay is placed onto a feed ground each morning to supply the nutritional needs of a 1,200-pound pregnant cow. Each cow will consume about thirty pounds of hay a day, and more if the temperature drops below zero. Ranching History of Ouray County of the Ridgway Public Library

Winter is, by necessity, a season of minimal outside work; we perform only the chores necessary for the survival and welfare of the livestock. It is also, for me, a season to relax, read, catch up my account books, and regain some of the weight and strength I lost over the summer and only partially recovered in the fall. Staying warm is a constant battle, but once warm, nothing is more wonderful than to hunker down and sleep like a bear. Deedee and I ski a few times through the season, but it is hard to find time when the cows must be fed every day. Also, because I work in the snow and the cold, I find that I'm not particularly excited about playing in it.

Finally, the cows will deliver their calves and the cycle will begin once again.

———•—•———

These work cycles, determined entirely by the weather and the seasons, define the enterprise known as ranching. It is not always glamorous work—putting down a horse with a broken leg or suffering frostbite while feeding livestock in a snow blizzard at thirty degrees below zero is hardly romantic. Nor is it remunerative work; the monetary reward rarely equals the physical effort and mental stress. In those years when the books show more red ink than black, I sometimes think the only things holding the ranch together, besides Deedee's supreme efforts, are baling wire and bag balm. But if you like working with animals (and we do) and don't mind outside work with heavy lifting, ranching can be very satisfying—satisfying because we can see, feel, and even smell the product of our labor, which is a part, however small, of the nation's food supply.

I hesitate to call what we do cowboy work because, as we have seen, ranching involves so much more than riding a horse. Also, the term *cowboy* has come to conjure up the romantic image of a man decked out in a bandanna, spurs, chaps, and big hat loping across an open meadow, rope flying, atop his trusty steed. In the background, provided by Hollywood and the mass media, are usually snow-capped mountains and a babbling brook in which can be seen a six-pack of the cowboy's favorite beer.

Because our culture wishes, for whatever reason, to romanticize and hence falsify the cowboy, we often fail to recognize what the men and women who work as cowboys actually do, why they do it, and what meager wages they receive for the hard life they live. Some cowboys say they do it because they like working outside and away from people. One cowboy I know said simply, "I can't do nothin' else." You can place as many descriptive adjectives in front of the noun as you want—rhinestone, drugstore, urban, rodeo, Hollywood, brown dirt, or cosmic—but cowboys remain hired laborers. They own neither the ranches they work on nor the cattle they work. In terms of not owning their own labor, they are little different from steelworkers in Pittsburgh or farm laborers in Salinas; in fact, cowboys are in a worse position because they are unprotected by a union. Far too often they earn less than the minimum wage and are asked to work in extremely dangerous conditions in the most severe weather, usually without medical insurance or retirement benefits.

Added to that is the fact that the traditional skills of the cowboy have become less important than formerly on the modern ranch. Ranchers today need the skills and technical expertise of computer programmers, animal nutritionists, agronomists, marketing specialists, and mechanics as well as horsemen. If ranch operators could hire individuals who combined all these skills, then we might have discovered and defined the modern, prototypical cowboy. Unfortunately, few cowboys today possess the education or experience to have developed these skills. Remembering the oft-repeated promise from the cowhand of yesterday, "If you can't do it from horseback, it ain't worth doin'," it is not surprising to hear the contemporary ranchers say with a certain degree of disrespect for the past, "Cowboys need not apply."

It is difficult for me to find good cowboys for the wages I can afford to pay. Why, they ask themselves, should they live away from their families, in a drafty mobile home or decrepit bachelor cow camp, while trying to raise a family on a thousand dollars a month and refried beans? The alternatives in Telluride, working on a construction site or attending a chairlift, grim though they may seem for someone raised on a ranch and skilled as a cowboy, are too often more attractive—and are certainly more remunerative.

Beneath the happy-go-lucky surface of virtually all the hired ranch workers I know is a serious and long-held goal to be an independent rancher. This goal of self-employment was and is the internal generator of hired labor in the rural West. But as all too many cowboys discover, it is no longer a realistic goal but a fading dream. The current recreational economy and the ever-increasing number of "urban cowboys" buying hobby ranches have inflated land prices throughout the Rocky Mountain West. I know of not a single instance where a ranch worker has traded his meager savings for an operating ranch.

We like to think of cowboys as independent and free-spirited people— "rugged individualists," to use the rejuvenated lingo of the day. But we know that is not true, recognizing as we do, I hope, that it is difficult to be a rugged individualist and a wage earner all in the same saddle.

Chapter Five

Visitors and Newcomers

There is nothing more American than loading the kids into a minivan, escaping the suburbs, and heading into the country for a two-week summer vacation. For many a vacationer from Hannover, Germany, to Hannibal, Missouri, the American West is the destination of choice.

The children are promised the opportunity to see, up close and personal, cowboys, Indians, and wild animals. The adults expect to witness spectacular landscapes or cast a fishing line in a mountain stream. Those coming from the East must suffer sleepless nights on lumpy mattresses after long days driving over a flat landscape on monotonous, gray ribbons of interstate concrete, broken only by intermittent stops for quarter-pounders. But just about the time the parents begin to question the wisdom of spending two weeks in minivan with the kids and think that maybe they should have sent them off to camp (if not to the kennel with the dogs) instead, the Rocky Mountains—the defining icon of the West—appear on the horizon. And once into the West, it is sometimes difficult for tourists to keep their minds on the trip's purpose in the face of all the billboards, brochures, and radio messages that bombard them. They are urged to visit any number of "authentic" Indian craft shops, "historic" forts, "live" shootouts, and "fun-filled" reptile ranches "just crawling with excitement."

There is a fascination with the memory of frontier violence, real or imagined, that attracts a constant pilgrimage of visitors, including many foreigners, to the American West. They come looking for places where cowboys, miners, outlaws, and other hard livers tamed a rugged frontier. Visiting the grave of that famous American idol Billy the Kid or locating a "restored" saloon where the "bullet holes can still be seen in the door" can be the highlight of a summertime search for the "real West." That visitors from the city seem always ready to accept, if not romanticize and embrace, nineteenth-century frontier gunplay while they simultaneously fear twentieth-century urban violence is not a logical inconsistency many rural Westerners recognize, much less wish to point out to tourists bearing Visa gold cards.

Most western towns today, even those whose existence barely predates the discovery of oil in the 1920s or uranium in the 1950s, have a tourist information center in an old railroad caboose or closed gas station to boost local attractions, however insignificant they may appear to the passing tourist. If there is nearby an exposed geologic formation, an abandoned mine, or the grassed-over ruts of an old emigrant trail, it is enough, the town fathers believe, to invest tax dollars in some poorly printed brochures. And if like most residents of western towns, especially mining towns, they believe their underground wealth was exported long ago to a distant region for the profit of big-city fat cats, they take immense pleasure, after much expense and imaginative effort, in stripping the fleeting tourists of their disposable dollars. What better way to compensate for past losses than with a little boosterism in the present.

Ouray's tourist trade, which would transform the city's economy in the late twentieth century, actually began in the late nineteenth century. It is to the credit of Ouray's merchants that, as early as the 1890s, they recognized the large profits that could be made not only from supplying the mines but from mining the tourists. In their efforts to attract Denver residents into the San Juans, and particularly to Ouray, the merchants, in conjunction with the Denver & Rio Grande Railroad, recognized that they had two very important assets: spectacular mountain scenery and a rail line to transport tourists to view it.

The railroad, anxious to diversify and increase its traffic beyond serving Colorado's struggling mining districts, began promoting several new resorts that were relatively close to Denver by rail—Colorado Springs, Central City, and Idaho Springs. And although Ouray lacked the attractions of those resorts, a trip into the remote San Juans was promoted as "an adventure on rails" for those who sought "health, wealth and the greatest scenery on earth." Highlighted in advertisements aimed at the new affluent urban middle class, whose members had both the money and the time for a two-week vacation in the mountains, were the two-hundred-foot Box Canyon Falls (adjacent to Ouray), local wildlife, and the mountain scenery of the San Juans.

In addition to the many travel books describing Colorado as an American Switzerland with mountain scenery and "bracing air," stories and engravings of Ouray appeared in Denver, Chicago, and New York newspapers. *Harper's Weekly*, with the assistance of Thomas Nast, the magazine's famous caricaturist and an enthusiastic visitor to Ouray—and the self-appointed publicity agent for the city—featured stories about the beauty of the San Juans accompanied by engravings based on the photographs of William H. Jackson. Along with the paintings of Thomas Moran and Albert Bierstadt, Jackson's photographs helped an increasing number of eastern tourists envision the Rockies.

The railroad ran excursion trains into Ouray throughout the summer months, including the Fourth of July holiday, when the locals put on a parade, water fight, and rock-drilling contest. The Denver & Rio Grande's popular Circle Route attracted thousands of summer visitors. Vacationers boarded the train in Denver, traveled south and west to Royal Gorge on the Arkansas River, and then, after changing trains in Salida, proceeded down the San Luis Valley to Alamosa and west across the Continental Divide to Durango, spending one night at the opulent Strater Hotel. The next day they rode the narrow-gauge line up the south side of the San Juans into Silverton and then on up to the small town of Ironton. Here passengers transferred to the Pioneer Stage Company's Concord coaches, which made the difficult and often dangerous eight-mile trip down the steep north side of the San Juans into Ouray. After a fine meal and an evening concert at the Beaumont Hotel, the tourists spent the night and departed the next morning, either for a side trip to Telluride or back to Denver by way of Montrose and the Black Canyon of the Gunnison River. Although Ouray was never as popular as more accessible mountain resorts such as Georgetown, Idaho Springs, and Glenwood Springs, an Ouray newspaper estimated that ten thousand Circle Route tourists visited the town in 1889.

Tourists came to Ouray not only for its daytime scenery but also for its nighttime entertainment, a fact that so irritated respectable residents that they undertook efforts to improve the moral tone of the city. In 1899, the editor of Ouray's *Solid Muldoon*, speaking no doubt for most miners, observed that if the ladies of Ouray "brought about prohibition, ended gambling, closed dance halls and houses of ill repute, why half the people and business interests would depart, leaving a dead town in its wake." In 1902, the ladies won a partial victory when the town closed the boisterous dance halls and gambling dens that were located within a short walk of the new railroad depot, but left open the city's numerous bars and brothels. Another Ouray paper, the *Ouray Times*, editorialized after the closings: "This marks the beginning of a new and more progressive era in the social conditions of Ouray. ... Dance halls are the product of new mining camps ... on the border of civilization." Having matured into a "respectable" city, Ouray had "long outlived the excuse for such institutions, if indeed, there ever was one."

Beginning in the late nineteenth century and continuing well into the third decade of the twentieth, Colorado gained a reputation as a place to recuperate from illness. Whatever the trouble—be it consumption, asthma, tuberculosis, nervous exhaustion, dyspepsia, or "general debility"—it could be cured by Colorado's dry air and abundant sunshine. Ouray's businessmen, always quick to recognize a new source of income, advertised the city as one of Colorado's finest health centers. Local entrepreneurs took advantage of the hot springs that lay directly beneath the town and opened "vapor caves." Advertised for their "medicinal properties and healing power," the hot springs attracted visitors from as far away as California. One bath, calling itself Sweet Skin Sanatorium, proclaimed that its "radio active" waters were a sure cure for everything, including neuralgia, rheumatism, blood disease, and problems of the liver. In 1926, the Radium Vapor Health Institute opened its doors in Ouray. The institute had private suites, a sweat room, individual cooling rooms, and a treatment center with a resident doctor and nurses. A slanted concrete floor led from the first floor to the vapor baths in the basement.

Hoping to compensate for the income lost as the fortunes of the mining industry declined, Ouray hotels began to advertise in Denver and eastern newspapers for summer visitors. Even after the dance halls were closed, the town's saloons and prostitutes continued to attract summer visitors from other areas of the state, especially Denver.

One enterprising entrepreneur with a family clientele in mind dug into the path of a hot spring and created a series of warm pools which he filled with goldfish. It became such a popular tourist attraction that he built another pool for two alligators, Allie and Gator. Always quick to promote itself, the city gave its blessing when someone had the idea of expanding the fishponds to a year-round public swimming pool. Under the direction of the Ouray Recreation Association, and with contributions from local merchants, the pool opened in 1926 with great fanfare as the goldfish and alligators looked on from their (separate) new homes next door.

The area's major attraction, however, remained its spectacular mountain scenery. As more people bought cars—first "touring" vehicles for the wealthy and later Mr. Ford's Model T for the masses—an increasing number of Kodak-carrying tourists made their way into the San Juans. Automobile drivers then as now found excitement and challenge in the narrow, winding mountain roads. Ouray became a major attraction because of its Million Dollar Highway, a narrow cliff-hanger of a road that rose out of Ouray up through Ironton Park and over Red Mountain Pass at 11,000 feet before descending into Silverton. The route, originally Otto Mears's old toll road built in the 1880s, was improved and extended over two additional mountain passes, Molas (10,900 feet) and Coal Bank (10,600 feet), and then on to Durango. To service the increasing number of vehicles, new filling stations appeared in the county, along with Ouray's first cottage court—the precursor to the modern-day motel. Just before the Depression struck, the city built a campground for these newly mobile tourists, who, for a small fee, received a twenty-four-hour guard service that allowed them to leave behind their personal belongings while they took day hikes into the mountains or went into town to see Al Jolson in *The Jazz Singer* at the Iris Theater.

Well into the 1970s, the tourist season was a short one. Summer visitors came in June and left by Labor Day. They owned little property, voted elsewhere, and expected nothing from Ouray County except a place to park a trailer, rent a cottage, eat a simple meal, and drink a beer. For the county, and especially for the town of Ouray, the tourists brought in dollars to replace the lost mining income. More motels and trailer parks appeared, long-closed restaurants reopened, and new curio shops opened their doors. Jeep tours into the mountains became increasingly popular. Tourists came to outnumber locals at the Fourth of July parade in Ouray and the Labor Day rodeo in Ridgway. The hot-springs pool, modernized once again in the 1950s, attracted well over a thousand visitors during the summer, and it soon began to attract a few off-season visitors, even without the alligators.

Some western towns in spectacular settings—places such as Sun Valley, Jackson Hole, Aspen, and Taos—served as summer residences for a few wealthy families and their friends. But because no captains of industry, no European royalty, nor any famous writers or artists summered in Ouray, the town lacked the cachet of the better-known vacation spots in the Rockies. Instead, Ouray attracted a new class of urban professionals who arrived by car or train for short visits. Starting in the 1960s and continuing today, the vast majority of summer visitors are working-class families who arrive in cars, jeeps, campers, and RVs, make few demands on the county's infrastructure or political leaders, and drop maybe a couple of hundred dollars into the local economy during a week's visit.

When MGM selected a ranch outside Ridgway as the location for the 1958 formula western *A Tribute to a Bad Man*, starring James Cagney, residents hoped the filmmaking industry would revive the fortunes of the dying town. Three years later, the studio returned to Ridgway to film a bigger movie, *How the West Was Won*, which starred Debbie Reynolds and Gregory Peck. Movie crews constructed false-front buildings, and existing town buildings—including the old bank and the railroad depot—received new names (the "Bank of Independence" and the "Independence Hotel") and much-needed facelifts. A few Ridgway ranchers hired on as extras to drive and man the wagons for the traditional Indian fight. With the local Ute Indians long since forcibly removed to Utah, Hollywood imported "Indians" from California and housed them at the town's rodeo ground.

Hollywood, always in love with its own romantic vision of the West, returned to Ridgway once again in 1968 when Paramount Pictures brought a large crew to film *True Grit*, with John Wayne in the role of the one-eyed Rooster Cogburn. But again Hollywood was dissatisfied with Ridgway's look, and again town buildings, at least those that had survived the dynamite explosion a few years earlier, were transformed into Hollywood's idea of a nineteenth-century frontier town. A local construction crew slapped some much-needed paint on the vacant Town Hall and gave the town a new name (Fort Smith), wooden sidewalks, and a false-front courthouse facing the town park, where a new gallows stood awaiting Hollywood hangings.

Locals still talk about the excitement of working as extras in the film ("the most damned excitement around here since that dynamite half destroyed the town"), and the opportunity to "be talkin' face to face with the Duke" is memorialized in framed photos that adorn ranch mantelpieces and the walls of the True Grit Café on the west side of the town park, where the Duke witnessed a triple hanging.

True Grit provided a temporary spike in the local economy, but in the long run it brought no new residents or tourists to Ridgway. With the departure of the film crew, Ridgway returned to its sleepy existence, having gained momentary notoriety, a new plastic-shingle roof for the post office, and a bell cupola atop the Town Hall. Not even Hollywood's discovery of Ouray County's breathtaking landscape or the Duke's Oscar-winning performance, however, could transform the place from an unknown mountain town to a major tourist attraction like Tombstone or Monument Valley. Tourists did not identify Fort Smith, a mythical western cow town in the mountains (not the one in Arkansas), with Ridgway. They had a hard enough time simply locating Ridgway in their Rand McNally road atlases.

In fact, the ranching community and the vast majority of county residents liked the county just the way it was—a small homogeneous community run by natives for natives. The handful of part-time summer residents interfered not at all with the workings of the county; and the few tourists, irritating as they might be in their shorts and hiking shoes, quickly passed through, depositing a few valuable dollars on the way.

The tourists in their funny outfits, however, were the vanguard of a fast and decisive change that would transform Ouray County completely in the 1980s. The county did not promote itself, did not invite change, and strongly resisted it when it came—partly because the change came so quickly, but even more because the growth came from an unexpected, although familiar, quarter. Residents expected growth in the region to come from the energy boom, but international events stopped short the anticipated invasion of drill rigs, retorts, and the people to man them.

Instead, growth came not from the energy sector but from a larger generator—an invigorated national economy that provided new levels of affluence and leisure to a growing managerial class. As corporate America expanded and continued its efforts to compete into the 1980s, companies offered their employees longer vacations, fat 401(k) accounts, early and often generous retirements, and, to their managers, large performance bonuses. An affluent leisure class that placed a high premium on personal health and recreation emerged. And these people sought refuge in rural areas far distant from the dangerous, crime-ridden, congested, and dirty inner cities where they received their paychecks, dividends, and bonuses.

As eastern and midwestern cities repelled people in the late 1980s with their crime, poor schools, and high taxes, Colorado's booming economy attracted new residents who fantasized about living in an American West where simple habits and old-time virtues still prevailed. New small companies sought a relatively inexpensive but trained labor force there, as did traditional industries such as manufacturing and food processing. Construction and service workers, professionals, and technical service personnel flowed into Colorado from California and the Midwest, areas of the country suffering from sagging economies. The revolution in telecommunications permitted professionals and "knowledge-based" entrepreneurs to conduct their business long-distance, through computer connections and easily accessible software.

More than half a million people moved into Colorado in the 1980s, attracted to the state by its physical beauty, strong job market, low tax rate, and healthy lifestyle in a clean and safe environment. In the ten years between 1982 and 1992, more than half a million acres of rural land, primarily along the Interstate 25 corridor between Fort Collins and Pueblo, was developed. Net migration into Colorado peaked in 1994 at seventy-two thousand individuals and afterward leveled off at about forty thousand a year.

People came to all the mountain states—to Arizona, Idaho, Montana, Nevada, New Mexico, Utah, and Wyoming as well as to Colorado. Dangling tax breaks and occasionally even free land, state economic development offices advertised to companies in the coastal states and the Rust Belt the advantages of moving to the progressive cities of the West: Denver, Albuquerque, Colorado Springs, Billings, Las Vegas, Phoenix, Tucson, Cheyenne. Just outside the region's livable urban centers were a host of first-class recreational opportunities—including skiing, hiking, and fishing—in an idyllic countryside where cattle outnumbered people, cowboys rode the range, and not a discouraging word was heard.

Between 1990 and 1996, the mountain states added almost 2.5 million people to their population—an 18 percent increase, three times the national average. Nevada grew an astounding 32 percent in those six years, Arizona 20 percent, and Colorado and Utah 16 percent. Colorado, the fifth fastest growing state in the nation, added another 600,000 people to its population between 1990 and 1997. The Rocky Mountain communities of Jackson Hole, Aspen, Vail, Steamboat Springs, Durango, Bozeman, and Santa Fe grew phenomenally as vacationers poured in, many of them affluent city dwellers who could afford the luxury of a second home in the Rockies. By 1996, Vail had the highest proportion (66 percent) of second homes of any resort town in the West.

Also between 1990 and 1996, 1.6 million more people moved to rural areas from cities and suburbs than migrated the other way. Ouray and the surrounding counties began to feel the effects of this great westering move to the countryside, which in part reflected the reverse of a long-standing nationwide rural-to-urban trend. Much of the area's growth began in the early 1980s, when Telluride, an old mining town, gained national recognition as a major ski resort. Along with this recognition came an affluent collection of Hollywood stars and corporate executives seeking second homes in a chic new hideaway. The population of San Miguel County has grown—exploded—almost 50 percent since 1990.

Every resort town has its halo effect. On the way to Florence, vacationers discover Fiesole, and the people in Fiesole find work as waiters in Florence. Basalt, Colorado, felt the effects of Aspen's growth, and Vail had a major impact on the small towns of Avon and Edwards.

Telluride too had a halo effect on its neighbors, particularly Ridgway, which was only forty miles to the east and closer to regular and more reliable air service to Denver than Telluride.

Ridgway immediately began to attract attention—first as a more affordable place to live than Telluride, and then as a rural area with its own beauty and charm. Increasing numbers of second-home buyers who desired close proximity to Telluride but did not want to live in the deep (and often dark) town valley or pay the escalating real estate prices looked to Ridgway, a town surrounded on three sides by distant mountains and close to some of the finest skiing, hiking, fishing, and scenery in the southern Rockies. Here one could live more economically and comfortably in a ranching community separate from, but convenient to, Telluride, with its glitzy lifestyle. Tourists, retirees, and corporate executives seeking summer retreats streamed into Ridgway. To service the new visitors and full-time residents came hundreds of new residents— hourly workers, small shopkeepers, construction workers, real estate agents, and others—all looking to catch a piece of the action.

The new residents filtered in from throughout the country, although it sometimes appeared that the vast majority were West Coast exiles soured on the California Dream. In the town's cafés, the clipped nasal tones of the upper Midwest mixed with Texas English, which can divide a one-syllable word into three distinct parts. Real estate agents scoured the countryside in search of new listings for property they could sell at prices unimagined six months earlier. Young singles, seeking not the new wealth in the area but the summer and winter pleasures of the mountains, came too. Some of the newcomers sought to change the county, its rules and mores; others accepted the place as they found it, content with its rather slow pace and relaxed lifestyle. These two groups, and their allies, would clash in the very near future.

Since 1975, the population of Ridgway and the surrounding area has more than doubled, from fewer than four hundred people to well over a thousand. Three mail carriers now deliver to almost five hundred rural post boxes, three times the number served by one carrier in the early 1970s. The town's post office, a dreary battleship gray prefab building erected in 1976, is barely adequate for the growing population. In the early 1970s, three Santa Clauses from the Elks Club would meet on Christmas Eve at the Little Chef bar to warm themselves and their helpers before delivering presents to children throughout the county. Now it takes twice as many Santas to perform the same community service. In 1986, it was possible to turn onto the highway at the town's main intersection without hesitation. Today, I must wait two or three minutes at the stop sign for the traffic to clear before moving into a constant flow of speeding eighteen-wheelers, pickups, cars, RVs, motorcycles, and trailers. And where Ridgway High School graduated two seniors in 1975 (the valedictorian and the salutatorian), today the school, even after a major physical expansion, is packed to capacity with more than three hundred students.

Old-timers no longer recognize the town. In the old rail yard, there stands a building housing a washateria, a real estate office, and an office supply shop. At the town's main intersection, two convenience stores with gas pumps have sprung up, as has the town's second liquor store. New shops and boutiques sit on the site of the old roundhouse. Local cappuccino cowboys can now find comfort at a coffeehouse while they ride herd on their stocks in the *Wall Street Journal.* Another new building to the rear of the coffeehouse is home to an outdoor equipment shop that sells ice-climbing equipment, kayaks, and a vast array of backpacks.

New shops up the street offer Guatemalan clothing and furnishings, fresh flowers, motorcycles, antique furniture and prints, lingerie, saddles, quilts, western wear, and "collectibles." Four restaurants serve everything from pasta, enchiladas, and lobster tails to alfalfa sprouts and zucchini bread. There's a new burger shop and a Subway franchise. A spacious and well-stocked grocery store, complete with lunch counter and video rentals, offers a butcher-manned deli and meat counter, fresh fruits and vegetables, and exotic foods in a variety that would have been inconceivable in 1975. At the new hardware store, household and ranch items are available at reasonable prices.

In the old bank building, there is a new library adjacent to an antique store and a shop that will design and remodel your "country" kitchen with marble-top counters and knotty pine cabinets. Fresh bread, coffee rolls, and deli sandwiches are available at a new bakery; and if you want your horoscope read or your back fixed, we have in residence an astrologer and a chiropractor. If the chiropractor doesn't remove the aches and pains, the hot-springs spa, the sacred spring once reserved by treaty for the Utes, is available. Bathing suits not required.

Across the highway on a site vacated by a small cattle ranch sits Trail Town, with its false-front facades and an array of "western" shops prepared to outfit the tourist in cowboy boots and a hat with the dimensions of a good-sized shade tree. If the newly attired tourist wants to mingle with "real" cowboys, there is a "western" bar next door; and when it's time to hit the sack, the new Super 8 Motel is just a few staggering steps away.

If you want a prefabricated ceiling truss, a four-hundred-dollar mountain bike, or an authentic buffalo-hide tepee, a shop in Ridgway can supply it. Visitors and residents no longer have to travel to Montrose to have their hair styled or to purchase a small boat to use at the reservoir. The welding shop can still fix a broken driveshaft on a baler; there's a shop to repair chain saws, and craftsmen who can remodel a house, build furniture, and create custom stained-glass windows. If you're looking for a tax accountant or a divorce lawyer, they too are available. And, of course, if it's land you want, we now have a dense pack of realtors (referred to as "dirt pimps" by some of my rancher friends) who will sell you a dream for "a reasonable price" and even arrange a balloon ride to show you your prospective spread.

In the 1970s, the only social organizations in Ridgway were the 4-H Club, the Rebeccas, the Sheriff's Posse, and the Volunteer Fire Department. Now there are clubs for those interested in books, investments, yoga, music, drama, and photography. The Performing Arts Guild sponsors a New York–based chamber group which offers a series of concerts each summer in Ouray; the renovated Sherbino Theater is the venue for plays and a lovely Christmas concert; a new dance hall over by Trail Town, built by local resident Dennis Weaver, hosts lively country-western dances throughout the year; and each summer the Ridgway Town Park, with its new gazebo and plantings, is home to an arts-and-crafts show. Forty miles away in Telluride there are separate summer festivals for devotees of jazz, film, chamber music, bluegrass, wine, and mushrooms.

The Rebeccas have moved to Ouray—their old building is now a sales office for mobile phones—but the Sheriff's Posse still meets in Ridgway, although no longer for law enforcement. Along with the Mountain Rescue Team, the posse now specializes in recovering stranded and lost hunters and hikers in the mountains. The Volunteer Fire Department, despite its increasing difficulty in soliciting volunteers, recently purchased a used fire truck for the new firehouse, upgrading their former equipment by about a half century. The Ridgway Chamber of Commerce advertises local business opportunities while promoting the advantages of western living in and around town.

A new bike and jogging path makes good use of the old rail line from Ridgway down to Montrose and past the new state park at the reservoir, where there are now picnic and camping sites, a boat rental facility, and a bait shop. The reservoir itself covers a former ranch; brown and rainbow trout now swim where cattle once grazed. Below the dam, the state has created a very popular catch-and-release fishing area for fly fisherman. The old fairground continues to be home to a local cowboy polo team and the roping club, both of which now include women. And throughout the summer, golfers play through eighteen holes and the deer at the Fairway Pines Country Club above town. After a dip in the club's indoor pool or a workout in the gym, meals and drinks are available at the clubhouse.

The Log Hill development typifies the massive changes affecting

Ridgway's ranching culture. In the early 1970s, an out-of-state investment partnership purchased almost two thousand acres of rangeland
west of Ridgway from a local rancher. The development is built on thin
clay soils amid cedar, piñons, and ponderosa pines on top of Log Hill, a
dry and rocky mesa overlooking the valley ranches along Dallas Creek
and Pleasant Valley. With its 180-degree views of the San Juans, Log
Hill is a dazzling setting for vacation homes, made all the more enticing
by the presence of a new eighteen-hole golf course. To solve the water
problem, the developers bought water rights from a local rancher, built
a pipeline and storage tanks, and ultimately received permission from
the water court in Montrose to divert water from Dallas Creek and
pump it four hundred feet up to Log Hill.

Log Hill, originally designed as a high-end recreational community
encircling a championship golf course, was slow to take shape. The roads
and infrastructure were completed in the face of considerable public
opposition within the county. Undercapitalized from the beginning, the
highly leveraged developers sold off multiple lots to other speculators,
who in turn sold individual lots to retirees, second-home buyers, and a
few local residents. By the mid-1980s, the number of permanent residents
equaled the number of seasonal residents. Today, retirees, professionals,
shop owners, and craftsmen live in comfortable homes (many of log
construction) with spectacular views of the Mount Sneffels Range to the
south and the Cimarron Range to the east. The golf course has yet to
attract its promised international clientele, but I see golf carts among
the grazing deer on crisp summer evenings.

A couple of miles away from a golf foursome, cattle graze in a
summer pasture belonging to a fourth-generation ranching family. The
ranchers have neither the time nor the inclination to play golf, or join
the country club. The ranchers do not know the golfers, nor do they
care to. The golfers don't know the ranchers, either, but they covet their
western lifestyle—without, of course, their "day job." Their spacious
mountaintop homes are filled with cowboy art, Indian artifacts, and

romantic novels about the West. They know a few people in town from their shopping in Ridgway or Ouray, but they know almost no one who works the ranches they overlook and understand little about the work that is performed on them. The golfers and the ranchers live side by side, in two different worlds.

Quite aside from their lifestyles, the two groups also see the world around them differently. A rancher looks at a meadow and sees hard work—an irrigation ditch that needs repair, noxious weeds beginning to appear, new rocks that will break a swather blade, and willows beginning to crowd out good grass. The summer resident looks at the same meadow and sees a passive and idyllic landscape, a rural painting of infinite beauty—and perhaps a useful winter or summer recreation area. An urban visitor to our ranch said a few years ago, as he looked out on one of my lush irrigated hay meadows, "What a beautiful golf course it would make." The idea of transforming my ranch into a golf course had never occurred to me, for the simple reason that I see the land as a workplace and not a playground.

The county's newer residents complain loudly if the expensive view they have just purchased is disturbed by a new building put up by a neighboring rancher or by a new power line or road. They want the county to stay just the way it was when they discovered it. One summer resident complained to me recently about the junkyard next to a neighboring rancher's house. I too found it something of an eyesore, but less so than this resident, who wished to report the visual pollution to the county commissioners as a violation of some unspecified regulation.

I know the junkyard and the owner, my neighbor, well. He worked for the railroad until it stopped running west over Dallas Divide to Dolores in the mid-1950s, and he never discards a piece of old equipment if he thinks it has any possible use—which, in his mind, it always does. Like many old-timers, he treats his machines like living creatures. As with the horses it replaced, he coaxes his tractor through its fieldwork. And like the horses, his machines have names like Big Boy and

Moses. A baler is attended to and doctored with the same care reserved for a good milk cow, and death, when it comes, is mourned, as if a 1949 baler had been a close member of the family.

I once rummaged through this junkyard looking for an old clutch plate that might work on a baler I had borrowed from another neighbor who was helping me put up some hay. "There's a world of spare parts in here," my neighbor said proudly. Another time, he found me a replacement door latch off an old Ford pickup that sat crippled next to his machine shop. My neighbor talked about an early-model John Deere tractor no longer in service as if he were reminiscing about a hired man since deceased: "That tractor gave me thirty-five years of devoted and reliable service. Only thing I ever did to it was change her fluids." An old rusted baler had been invaded for a chain sprocket, and yet another injured pickup (an International) without its left front wheel served as a rich supply for leaf springs, a gearbox, and a hard-to-find starter switch ("Company don't make 'em anymore, so she got some value to her," he said). "I suppose I could get rid of some of this stuff," my neighbor once admitted, "but where could I take it? Hell, I kinda like looking at it ... reminds me of some good folks and better days."

I mentioned all this to my summer neighbor, but I never could get her to share my ranching friend's aesthetic vision. Nor did she appreciate another neighbor of ours placing a double-wide mobile home within view of her property. "Is there nothing we can do?" she asked me. "Not much," I responded in sympathetic frustration. My standing as a defender of beautiful vistas unmarred by man-made structures had been somewhat compromised by my own actions. I had been the recipient of harsh criticism for selling off some acreage I owned adjacent to the cemetery, where there immediately appeared a not very attractive mobile home. I didn't like the new double-wide just over my south fence any more than I liked the older mobile home adjacent to the cemetery for which I was indirectly responsible. But in a sense I had to agree with my mobile-home neighbor, who said curtly when confronted with our neighbor's complaint that his double-wide interrupted her beautiful vista of Mount Sneffels, "If you don't like it, don't look at it." It is not easy to maintain beauty in paradise.

Not far from the junkyard and mobile homes, but out of sight of them, are ranches recently purchased by summer residents. Up the valley sits the ranch once owned by Marie Scott, born in the county at the turn of the century to a father who raised cattle along East Dallas Creek and on Sundays rode circuit for God in the mining towns of the area. To help support the family, his wife taught at the one-room schoolhouse just over Dallas Divide to the west, a hard seven-mile ride from the ranch. Marie, along with her sister, Lorraine, learned firsthand the rigors and skills of ranching. Ever one to save her earnings, Marie made her first land purchase with money that came from the sale of horse hay to the mines in Ouray. An astute businessperson with a keen eye for good cattle and productive land (and owners in debt), Marie purchased, usually with cash, thousands of acres sold for taxes in the 1920s and 1930s. Some say the only reason Marie ever married was to get her hands on her husband's good Hereford herd, which she did after their very brief marriage. In her lifetime, Marie traded thousands of acres with other ranchers and the government. It's said that in one trade with the United States Forest Service, Marie cut the timber off a good-sized parcel before trading it back to the government for some better timbered land adjacent to her ranch. Her fences were the best in the country—straight, tight, and long-lasting. She earned a reputation for honesty and hard work and expected the same of her peers. She once said she wouldn't "hire a man who wears waist overalls or smokes. If he isn't pulling up his pants, he's rolling a cigarette." At one time, Marie had assembled well in excess of 150,000 acres covering an area from Ridgway eighty miles west to the Utah border. In Ridgway, Marie had bought out old homesteads that still, for the old-timers, are familiar names: the Brown place, the Harrison place, the Lewis, Sherbino, Baumgartner, Anderson, Nelson, Williams, Cuddington, Krontenburg, and Vance places.

Marie Scott, the county's largest landowner in the mid-twentieth century. Here she poses with a member of the cast of the movie *The Unsinkable Molly Brown*, filmed on her Ridgway ranch in 1964. Ranching History of Ouray County of the Ridgway Public Library

When she died, in 1979, Marie left most of her land to friends and people who had worked for her around Ridgway. For years, I leased from one of her close associates almost ten thousand acres of summer pasture she once owned in neighboring San Miguel County, beautiful range country of open parks and aspen groves that we all referred to as "Marie's Summer Country." We purchased from her estate a small parcel of irrigated meadow in the valley adjacent to our ranch. The heart of her ranch empire is currently the headquarters of the fourteen-thousand-acre Double RL Ranch, owned by Ralph Lauren, the clothing designer out of New York City.

Marie's ranch is now a showplace, the backdrop for feature articles in fashion magazines about the "magical allure" of the American West. The ranch has homes for workers, guests, and the owner. Its amenities include a swimming pool and a stable for classic antique race cars. The Double RL Ranch is a well-managed working cattle ranch and a significant economic asset to the county. It employs a full array of cowboys, irrigators, mechanics, cooks, and housekeepers, and its corrals, sheds, fences, barns, cattle, and vehicles are the envy of any rancher. It has been meticulously and expensively remodeled by its owner to provide a backdrop image for his enormously successful line of western clothes and furnishings. A typical cattle ranch it is not.

One of Marie's neighbors in Pleasant Valley was Harry McClure, born in 1899 in the cabin built by his father, Americas McClure, a homesteader who came to Ridgway from the Midwest with his uncle in the late 1880s. With his firsthand knowledge of cattle, Harry built on his inheritance. His Hereford calves brought premium prices at sales throughout Colorado and Kansas, and with those profits, and a little assistance from his Thursday night poker games, he slowly added to the size of Pleasant Valley Ranches by buying out neighboring homesteads. Harry gained his reputation through his deeds rather than his words, although when he spoke in his slow and measured manner, people listened. About the only thing that angered Harry was a stray dog in the middle of his cattle. Usually clad in bib overalls, he walked with a slight limp, the result of having been struck by lightning along a fence line many years back. The strike knocked the soles off his boots and the buckle off his belt and left him temporarily paralyzed from the waist down, but he dragged himself to his jeep, got it started without using the clutch, and drove through some fences to get help. He never did find his belt buckle. Like his neighbor Marie, when he gave his word, he always and without fail delivered on it. Harry and Marie and others of their generation were content to let their neighbors judge them not by what they possessed but by who they were—good neighbors and honest and hardworking men and women.

Late one October afternoon, after a very dry summer, Harry asked me if I had any hay for sale. I said yes, about ninety tons, and without much discussion we settled on a price of fifty-five dollars per ton, the going rate at the time. He said he'd pay me half now and the other half in the spring. We shook hands on it and went on to discuss the cattle market over a beer. In the course of the conversation, I asked Harry if he would consider selling the old Sneva place, a 240-acre ranch Harry had bought back in the 1930s from the German-born rancher who had the run-in with Ridgway's Hundred Percent American Club. The Sneva Ranch, which was about six miles away from Harry's outfit, had some superb hay meadows and water rights and adjoined my ranch along Dry Creek. "No," he said, "don't think I could do that right now ... but maybe sometime."

Harry McClure with his mother, circa 1930. The Hereford cattle off Harry's large ranch always brought premium prices at the Denver and Kansas City stockyards. Ranching History of Ouray County of the Ridgway Public Library

A year and a half later, the Internal Revenue Service informed me that my tax return was going to be audited. The auditor, who came up from Grand Junction and knew nothing about cattle, hay, irrigation, or any other part of ranching as far as I could tell, questioned me about some hay sales, including my sale to Harry a year and a half earlier. "So where's the contract?" he asked. "There is no contract," I responded. He looked at me as if I had just fallen off the onion truck. I had made a $5,000 sale without a contract? I informed the incredulous IRS agent that we didn't use contracts around here, at least not with ranchers we knew, and that I had made the hay transaction with a handshake. I suggested he call Harry, which he did. Harry, of course, confirmed what I had said but forgot to tell the agent that he had paid me for ninety-two tons because he'd weighed some of the bales and figured they weighed a bit more than I had originally estimated. I later apologized to Harry for the inconvenience of the IRS call. I told him the audit had occurred on the occasion of my daughter's fourth birthday party and that I believed it was the first time an IRS agent had ever been made to play Pin the Tail on the Donkey. Harry said, "I trust you used the IRS ass as the object."

Later that same year, I encountered Harry at the café and asked if he'd given any more thought to selling the Sneva place. "Maybe we better talk about it," Harry said. I suggested he come up to the ranch the next day for dinner and jokingly suggested we play a game of pool for the Sneva property. Harry arrived at the appointed hour in his usual outfit: bib overalls, cowboy boots cracked on the outside edges, and a battered, sweat-stained straw hat. He was at this time over eighty and had a slight tremor in his hands, and his bloodshot eyes drooped toward his rosy cheeks and wide grin like a basset hound's. "What about a game of eight-ball?" Harry immediately suggested. I nodded toward the table and racked up the balls, fearing all the while that my playful suggestion about shooting for the Sneva property might be taken seriously, especially if I lost. Harry elected to go first, and within five minutes he had cleaned the table and humiliated me. "Well," he said, "I've decided to sell the Sneva." I immediately offered him a cash price, which he immediately rejected, suggesting a higher, but not unfair, one. "Can't take a penny less," he stated. Clearly it was take it or leave it; of course, I took it.

Harry passed away in 1988, leaving his cattle and land (approximately ten thousand acres) to his heirs. Saddled with a huge tax burden and unwilling to continue the cattle operation, his heirs sold parcels to developers, who in turn created "ranchettes." Today, new homes and their residents overlook Harry's hay meadows. The heirs sold most of the ranch to the owner of a satellite dish company from Denver. The ranch is a shell of its former self, and the McClure heirs are now dispersed in occupations and locations far distant from the land and the chores of tending to a herd of eight hundred mother cows.

Other pioneer ranches have changed hands, too, bought with urban money by people seeking privacy, a vacation retreat, a tax advantage, or a land investment. The cattle that graze these ranches are not always of primary concern to the owners, although they may be to the IRS. As decorative objects that give definition to the mountain scenery and its foreground, the cows and calves keep the grass mowed while providing their owners with convenient tax write-offs against income earned elsewhere. Legal fees, clothing sales, oil royalties, car sales, satellite dishes, and superior corporate performances sustain and pay for these cattle ranches, not the sale of hay or beef cattle. And it is certain that ranch profits do not pay for the private jets that transport the new owners and their friends between their permanent homes and these summer ranch retreats.

A pioneer ranch outside Ridgway bought by a Los Angeles lawyer in the 1960s was recently donated to Stanford University, which then sold it to an Ohio financier. Another Ohioan, an industrialist, assembled three adjoining ranches into a beautiful vacation retreat. A wholesale car and truck dealer from southern California put together his "spread" by purchasing four pioneer ranches. One old-time ranching family sold their land to a developer in exchange for a larger operation in Baggs, Wyoming. Their former hay meadows on the edge of Ridgway, subsequently incorporated into the town, are now the site of the Super 8 Motel, a new apartment complex, and mini mall. A Texas oilman who summers in Ridgway on one of his many ranch properties is now one of the largest landowners in the entire three-county area. The property of an old-time Ridgway rancher who died recently is currently on the market at a price that cattle sales could never pay for. The largest acreages now belong to owners whose money is harvested in the city and transferred to land in Colorado.

All in all, well over half of the forty or so original pioneer ranches in the county that were operated by the same family for at least two, and in some cases four, generations have now been broken up and sold outside the family. Some of the folks ranching when we arrived in the early 1970s continue to do so now. Members of the Wolford, Adams, Weber, Collin, Jutten, Lowry, Hudson, Ary, and Hutt families can be seen every summer day irrigating their hay meadows. Jack Potter's sons maintain the family's excellent Hereford herd, and the Ingos continue to run cows on the edge of town and on Log Hill after their uncle, an original homesteader, passed away more than a decade ago. Gertrude Perotti's ranch still runs a few cattle and sheep, just as it did at the turn of the century. Roger and Gail Noble still have their small sheep and cattle operation.

The Soderquist ranch and farm in Colona has been in the same family for over a century, surviving through hard work and meticulous budgeting of limited resources. "To make a farm work," Andy Soderquist said in *The Way It Was*, "you have to do it yourself. ... You can't hire labor. It's hard to farm with hired labor and make it pay." Esther Lewis, whose father homesteaded our ranch, oversees a small cattle operation north of town by the reservoir. Well into her nineties now, she finds it difficult to take her weekly horseback ride to inspect her yearling steers grazing up against the base of Mount Sneffels. "The seventies were a breeze," Esther said recently, "but in the eighties I've had to slow down a bit."

Those who continue to ranch for a living do so out of habit and a love of livestock, and, in some instances, for lack of other work. Raising cattle is the only business they know, and they'd be hard put to change their place of work much less their occupation without additional skills.

Ridgway is a changed place. Llamas now graze within sight of Americas McClure's homestead, and a home built of Italian marble with an interior finished in exotic woods imported from South American and African rain forests overlooks land assembled by Marie Scott, whose modest frame dwelling now houses hired help at a ranch whose fences cost more than most older valley ranchers will earn in a lifetime. Other trophy homes, log and fieldstone cathedrals with illuminated elk antler chandeliers, dot the countryside. No longer an isolated region of hardscrabble ranches, the county is slowly changing to a chic landscape where cattle and sheep, and the old-timers who tend them, are mere decorative objects seen through the windshields of passing Hummers and BMWs.

Chapter Six

Community Fragmentation

The first spring on our ranch we learned quickly that we should not expect a visit from the Welcome Wagon. That we had moved to Ridgway not merely from out of state but from New York City was all the more reason, in the eyes of our neighbors, that we should be looked on with suspicion, if not disrespect. When, for example, I told my neighbor, the president of the ditch company, that I needed an additional twelve hours to repair a large irrigation box in the Dallas ditch before he turned in the water for the season, he disregarded what I thought was a perfectly legitimate request and opened the headgate anyway. The next morning, I found that my tools had been carried away by the water and my irrigation box was still inoperable.

I thought it would be good to have a chat with my neighbor. In retrospect, I probably came on a bit strong when I opened the conversation by suggesting he was a first-class son-of-a-bitch and if he wanted to play games I was perfectly capable, and damned well willing, to respond in kind. Very calmly my neighbor explained to me not only the ways of the ditch company ("We always turn the water on by the first week in May") but also his and no doubt other ranchers' image of folks from the city. In essence, he said: "As a newcomer you don't understand how we work around here; and as an outsider from the city, you'll probably never understand." Over the years my neighbor and I have come to understand and even appreciate each other. But suspicion of newcomers and dislike of outsiders, particularly those from the city, are ingrained in Ouray County, and throughout much of rural America.

To be tagged both a newcomer and an outsider is indeed a heavy burden to carry in a rural county. A newcomer can never become an old-timer, of course, but he or she can escape the "outsider" epithet by accepting—or at least not criticizing—the value system of the longtime residents. A major component of acceptance, although by no means a guarantee, is for the outsider to share the age-old rural dislike of the city.

Ouray's County's longtime residents looked on the new residents in the early 1980s as somehow inferior beings, not because they were less educated or poorer (which on average they were not), but because, for the most part, they had moved to the county from cities where crime, sexual permissiveness, and corruption prevailed. Anyone who came from such evil places, even if not born there, was by association greeted with deep suspicion. And city people were too burdened with useless knowledge to act rationally on their own behalf in the country. Like delinquent children, they had to be protected and educated to the ways of the rural West. If in the end the city folk didn't wish to conform to the ways of Ouray County, well, that was their problem. There would be no compromise with urban values and no slack given to city slickers.

Deedee and I also came to understand during our first summer on the ranch that attached to this denigration of the city and city folk was a macho attitude of superior toughness that assumed that those of us who moved into the county from cities lacked the backbone, and certainly the skills, to survive the rigors of the Wild West. As someone whose survival skills had been honed by mountain training in the army, a stint as a war correspondent in Vietnam and Laos in 1970, and a couple of muggings on New York's Upper West Side, I kept quiet about the implicit suggestion that anyone not born on a ranch in the West was a wimp.

The old-timers' attitude of yeoman superiority and their deep-seated suspicion of all outsiders structured and influenced the county's internal debates over land use, the direction of the Ridgway school, and, more generally, differing lifestyles. Beginning in the 1980s, when the county experienced a 30 percent increase in population and its longtime residents felt challenged by a foreign value system brought in (almost like a virus) by newcomers, the debates caused considerable social fragmentation. It was a disruptive experience common to many rural western counties along the spine of the Rockies.

Two very distinct groups of newcomers moved into Ouray County, bringing with them two very different sets of expectations. Some were attracted to the area by what immigrants to the West have always sought: opportunity—a better job, a healthier lifestyle, maybe even a new beginning in a place where, in William Kittredge's words, "you can have a shot at being what you want to be." By California and East Coast standards, living expenses and taxes were low, the environment clean, and the schools free of drugs, and the only congestion occurred at the post office while residents waited for the mail to be sorted. The local sheriff, Art Dougherty, bragged that no major crime had occurred in the county for more than three decades and advised newcomers, as he had advised me when I arrived in 1974: "Son, there are only three things you need to remember around here. Stop at all stop signs; signal when you turn; and if you hunt deer out of season, be sure you eat 'em." With a spacious and free playground of public land right outside every door, Ouray County was an immensely attractive area to those seeking to rejuvenate a life gone sour because of a weak marriage or a boring job. Never mind that jobs were scarce here; with a bit of ambition, perseverance, and pluck, one could attain happiness in the new country.

In addition, Ouray County also attracted a more affluent, but far smaller, group of part-time residents who sought sanctuary in the open spaces. Like the European aristocracy of the eighteen and nineteenth centuries, America's corporate elite sought solace on country estates from their hectic but profitable lives in the cities. When this nation was younger, the managerial class looked for escape in the countryside and shores surrounding New York, Chicago, Boston, and Detroit. But once-rural areas on Long Island, in New Jersey, and along the Great Lakes filled up with people and became cluttered with the same problems the leisure seekers were trying to avoid.

By contrast, the rich saw the West, with its immense size and relatively inexpensive land, as an area where they could carve out their own exclusive, private preserves in virgin wilderness. Here, in the process of buying a lifestyle, one could capture a dream—that of owning a "spread" where only trees and open meadows interrupted the eye as it sought the setting sun. With both time and money to travel the long distances necessary to enjoy their extended vacations, an increasing number of captains of industry sought refuge in the Rocky Mountains from Montana to New Mexico. In the 1930s, the Rockefeller family bought into Jackson Hole, Wyoming, and Averell Harriman and his friends selected Sun Valley, Idaho. Today, with transportation no longer a problem, a far larger wealthy class enriched by a five-year boom in the stock market is seeking private land reserves in the relatively sparsely populated open West.

According to *Worth* magazine, in 1997, one hundred individuals and families owned a bit more than 1 percent of the nation's acreage, holdings that add up to a land mass the size of Kentucky. Henry Singleton, cofounder of the Teledyne Corporation, owns cattle ranches in central and southeastern New Mexico that together total more than a million acres. Media mogul Ted Turner, the nation's largest private landowner, owns another million acres in New Mexico. Together the state's two largest private landowners control more that 3 percent of New Mexico's private land. Among Turner's current holdings are eight ranches and three plantations in Montana, New Mexico, Nebraska, Florida, Georgia, and South Carolina. His advice for those looking to invest in land: "Go West. You can get a lot of acres cheap. Stay out of New England because there are too many people there." On his future land strategy, Turner observed: "Well, I'm trying to fill in. You ever make puzzles as a kid? First, you put the corners in. Then you try to get the border done. And then you try to fill in. So I've got property on both coasts and in Montana, which is on the Canadian border, and in New Mexico, which is a Mexican border state. Now I'm trying to fill in." There are those who wonder if Turner, who once said, "If I want to save the West, I'll have to buy it," will be looking to Colorado as the next piece in his land puzzle.

A number of wealthy families came into Ouray County seeking to fulfill their own land dreams. Their habits and lifestyles clashed almost immediately with those of the farmers and ranchers who lived on the land adjacent to them. The newcomers were not accustomed to "neighboring," the time-honored tradition of working together so necessary among ranchers with limited resources. Nor did they understand nature's time; they continued to live urban lives run by the industrial clock rather than by the seasons. Accountants, not the sun, designed their working day. They woke, worked, and slept to a different schedule; and, confined to inside work and the dictates of the bottom line, they comprehended neither the rhythms of the seasons, the limitations of weather, nor the debilitating fatigue of muscle power. Their understanding of stock extended to IBM and General Motors, not to Hereford and Angus. A Limousin was a long, sleek vehicle that took one to work and later to the theater, not a French breed of cattle. The food chain was to them an abstraction. Milk came from Safeway, cereal from Kellogg, and fifty-seven assorted other things from Heinz. They carried with them a vague sense that everything "natural" was "organic," and hence safe, and anything that didn't fit into those vague categories was either unfit for human consumption or, at a minimum, unhealthy.

Wealthy urban families sought in the countryside respite from their city lives. For them, fatigue came not from physical exertion on the job but from the mental stress associated with the challenges of high finance. They got their exercise in private athletic clubs or at exotic international spas and resorts. They liked to jog, go to the theater, attend museum openings, and, if time allowed, serve on charitable boards that helped ameliorate the injuries caused by the harsh dictates of the Darwinian economy from which they had so handsomely profited. The rich carried with them a supreme confidence that the value of their material possessions (earned or inherited) was directly related to their superior intelligence and ability to meet the challenges of modern-day capitalism. And they brought into the countryside a supreme confidence—critics called it arrogance—that their talents, so appropriate for urban deal making, could be transferred to rural life.

Their Ridgway neighbors were, in a sense, precapitalists—people who measured their worth not by material possessions but by physical skills and personal experiences, on which they, if asked, could place no quantitative value. A day working cattle on horseback, a well-crafted barn, or a properly irrigated hay meadow counted for far more than owning, or bragging about, a large ranch or bank balance. Local ranchers took life as it came to them, with no sense of entitlement. Whatever they considered their due came from hard work, God's blessing, and a bit of luck.

The Hollywood and Wall Street ranchers who bought spreads near Jackson Hole, Aspen, Livingston, Bozeman, and even Ridgway in the 1980s were immediately identifiable by their shiny new pickups and the private planes parked at nearby airports. One of Colorado's new ranchers arrives in a private Gulfstream jet that is accompanied, like a pilot fish, by a smaller jet for the backup crew. While the owner vacations at his ranch for a month, the flight crews fly houseguests and business associates back and forth from the owner's home city. Of course, the cost of operating the jets is a legitimate business expense of the ranch or of the company where the corporate cowboy makes his living.

The new breed of ranchers can also be immediately identified by their clothes. A tooled leather belt with a silver buckle emblazoned with the ranch brand holds up artificially faded, and sometimes pressed, designer jeans, which have just the right cut around the hips and seat and are tucked into high-topped, hand-made, exotic leather boots. The

Stetson hat, preferably with sweat stains at the base of the wide brim that blend in with the expensive silver or braided horsehair band, is worn at a jaunty angle. A faded jean jacket, or perhaps a ragged leather one, might be slung casually over the shoulder in the event a storm, or more likely a camera, should appear. The intended visual effect is the Marlboro Man—but most definitely without the Marlboro.

For dinner parties at the ranch or fund-raisers in Aspen, Denver, Jackson, or Vail, the women, too, get gussied up in "cowboy couture." The *Denver Post* recently described what the well-dressed cow person would be wearing this season: "Expect chic cowgirls duded up in suede shirts with hand-painted western motifs; velvet broomstick skirts; jackets with fringe and beading; and belts and baubles in sterling silver and turquoise. For men, West-dressed means vests in tooled leather or tapestry with decorative buttons; horsehair braided bolo ties; and formal morning coats." Nice items if you can afford them, but a bit pricey, if not impractical, for the average rancher, whose idea of dressing up is a clean pair of jeans. Ralph Lauren, the owner of one of Ridgway's largest ranches, launched the high-fashion western look in 1978 with a collection that featured petticoats and prairie skirts, Navaho blanket wrap skirts, and fringed leather jackets.

It is resentment, not envy, that separates old-line ranchers from the chic new variety frequently the Rocky Mountain West. For more than a century, local ranchers never had to concern themselves with outside competition for the area's land. They bought and sold and leased ranchland among themselves based on the price of livestock. When cattle prices shot up, ranchers waited for the inevitable seven-year cycle to adjust prices downward before thinking about a land purchase. The two-legged stock market—the one on Wall Street—had no bearing on land prices in Ouray, nor did the price of oil in Texas or gold prices in London.

At first, the summer tourists had no wish to buy land; they wanted only to hike or camp on it, and then return home. Well into the late 1970s, the value of a ranch was determined by its water rights and hay-growing capacity. If, for example, a twelve-hundred-acre ranch had the summer grass and winter hay capacity to run three hundred cows in a normal year, and a prospective buyer was willing to pay $2,000 a cow unit (about average in the 1970s), the value of the ranch property was placed at $600,000 or $500 an acre. Snow-capped mountains in the background and a babbling brook in the foreground did not increase a ranch's productive value, nor did the cows concern themselves with the visual amenities of a property, caring only that the grass and water be plentiful.

But about the time of the big-money invasion in the early 1980s, a number of things happened to change both the economics of ranching and the attractiveness of owning a ranch. First, Americans began to be barraged by messages telling them not only that they were overweight but also that their diet contained too many saturated fats. Experts on morning talk shows urged consumers to lay off red meat, especially beef, to substitute a chicken breast or a filet of sole for a juicy T-bone. Annual per capita beef consumption dropped from more than ninety pounds a year to less than seventy over a period of five years. Beef prices fell off precipitously in the late 1970s and early 1980s as health-conscious Americans, particularly affluent urbanites, eschewed beef for fowl, fish, and pasta.

The cattle industry was slow to adjust to the change in consumer preferences. Beef production continued at record levels while chicken, pork, and fish captured a larger and larger share of the consumer dollar. To remain in the beef business, cattlemen were forced to cut their animal-unit production costs by either capturing savings in larger units of production (bigger ranches) or paring expenses in their current operation. In Ridgway, however, almost all the ranchers had already cut their operating expenses to the bone. To save money, ranchers deferred purchasing new breeding stock, repairing fences, purchasing a new baler, or giving the hired man a raise. The alternative of expanding their cattle operations disappeared with the decline in their incomes and the increased cost of land in the valley.

In the early 1980s, as the West in general and Ouray County in particular became an increasingly more attractive place to play, invest, and live, vast amounts of local ranchland changed hands. For centuries, the San Juans had remained relatively remote and unspoiled (travel magazines called them "undiscovered"), but those with money and time and private jets found it quite accessible. Ralph Lauren purchased his twelve-thousand-acre ranch in 1980 after only a few local ranchers could afford to buy some of the smaller parcels from Marie Scott's estate. A Texas oil family bought four Ouray County ranches, including one adjoining ours, and then purchased at public auction more than five thousand acres of Marie's high-country summer range. Other large ranches changed hands when longtime ranching families, tired of battling long winters and low prices, sold to out-of-state buyers seeking Colorado cattle ranches within sight of the mountains.

As land prices continued to escalate, more and more old-time ranchers sold out and either moved their outfits elsewhere or retired. One rancher I know said he wanted to get as far away as possible from the "instant" ranchers and their "duded up outfits" who surrounded him. They "didn't pay their dues," the old-timer explained to me, "by having to suffer the lean years. Now they think they're cattlemen just because they sold some oil in Texas and bought a herd of fancy overpriced cows at the sale barn. And with their money, they can buy themselves out of dumb mistakes." His resentment of hobby ranchers was surpassed only by his contempt for a government that allowed, indeed encouraged, "big hats with big bucks" to exist in the cattle industry.

The old-timers who remained in Ouray County still set its rules and standards, but these came under increasing attack as the newcomers sought more services, bigger and better schools, and major changes in the land-use regulations. Growth, with all its attendant problems, hit the county hard and fast.

———·—·———

Developers did not (and do not) have an easy time of it in Ouray
County. In the early 1980s, the county commissioners (a Colona
rancher and two Ouray businessmen, all longtime residents of the
county) recognized that something would have to be done to control
the size and location of new homes and businesses. "Will it be cows
or condos?" the local newspaper asked in an editorial, suggesting the
parameters of a major debate in the county.

The county already had in place land-use regulations that were, by
Colorado standards, both unique and tough. These regulations, passed
in the 1970s, established three zones: valley, foothill, and alpine. Development was encouraged only in the foothill zone, which comprised dry
hillsides or mesas that had little grazing value to the ranchers but were
still suitable for houses. In this zone, developers could, after putting in
roads, water, sewage, and electric lines, and with the county's approval,
build to an average density of one unit per five acres. Houses had to be
hidden by trees, away from the skyline, and off the irrigated meadows,
which, along with the forested mountains, accounted for the county's
visual beauty. In the alpine zone and in some places adjacent to national
forest land, development was limited by Mother Nature (climate and
topography), in conjunction with the county regulations. Unlike other
heavily forested counties in the West, Ouray's timber had not been cut
over, and no ugly stumps cluttered the landscape, as they do in much of
Montana and the Pacific Northwest. In both alpine and valley zones,
the county set a density limit of one living unit per thirty-five acres.

As the pressure to liberalize these regulations increased in the
1980s, the county commissioners, with the assistance of the Ouray
County Planning Commission, considered revising the land-use codes
and regulations. There was growing evidence that some of the county's

streams were being contaminated by sewage. The location and design of septic systems needed to be tightened, as did the building and electrical codes. The debate over whether or not to liberalize the allowable density in the valley and alpine zones attracted the most attention. When two developers announced plans to build a ski resort on a north-facing slope just beneath Mount Sneffels and high-density housing on property once owned by Marie Scott, county citizens crowded into a public hearing at the Ridgway School to voice their strong opposition.

With the support of the county commissioners, the Planning Commission, of which I was chairman, polled all residents about whether or not they wanted major changes in the county's land-use regulations. The commission wanted to determine whether county taxpayers preferred no growth, uncontrolled growth, or limited growth, and if the latter, what kind and with what sanctions. It turned out, not surprisingly, that the vast majority of citizens wanted to preserve the county's beauty while simultaneously allowing limited growth. How that was to be accomplished they could not tell us.

In the public hearing that followed the survey, developers argued that with growth came jobs and a corresponding increase in the tax base. Real estate interests, including brokers, salesmen, and a few ranchers who wished to maximize their land value by selling off unproductive land for subdivided ranchettes, wanted free rein to do with private property whatever the market allowed. Opposing any restrictions on size, location, or design of development, those in favor of a laissez-faire policy saw the possibility of huge profits as more and more people discovered the beauty of the county and made plans to buy land, either for immediate use or for future speculation. To a large extent, the real estate brokers were betting (correctly, as it turned out) that demand for land in Ouray County would increase the per acre value over time—and sooner rather than later.

Many county residents (new and old) who wanted to see more jobs— for themselves and for their children—allied themselves with the pro-growth realtors. The county needed jobs, they argued with considerable logic (in the mid-1980s Ouray had one of the highest unemployment rates in the state), and neither agriculture nor mining could be expected to provide them. Rather than devising new regulations to further burden developers, they said, the county should encourage new businesses and inexpensive housing, including light industry and mobile home parks.

Opponents of unrestricted development, including many retirees and summer people, countered by charging that the developers were making false promises. They were land speculators interested in making a fast buck, said their critics—here today and gone tomorrow, with no care for how or where they scarred the countryside with their mobile home parks and housing tracts. Growth would mean higher, not lower, taxes to pay for new schools, roads, and public services. The opponents also charged that the upscale "affordable" houses the developers were bragging about were not designed, and certainly were not priced, for locals; they were intended for the second-home market—an inducement to unwanted and unnecessary growth. A few no-growth advocates argued that residents wouldn't be debating the growth, no-growth issue in the first place if it weren't for some newcomers with limited skills and meager resources coming in and wanting to change the county to meet their needs. We were doing just fine, they said, until the newcomers wanted to change the rules.

The positions of the various groups on the growth issue tended to be fairly predictable, although not in every instance. The more affluent residents, particularly the hobby ranchers, wanted the county closed to further development. To a large extent, they confirmed the old adage that "the last one in wants to close the door." Aesthetic concerns defined their arguments. Tract houses and mobile homes, and the roads and power lines to serve them, would desecrate the landscape and destroy the beauty that had attracted them to the county in the first place. The present and future value of the county lay in its beauty, they argued, and any further development would only depreciate that value. Self-interest was also at work, of course, since these landowners (some with more than a thousand acres) recognized that unplanned, uncontrolled, and unattractive development would adversely affect their own property values. And those who came to the county as summertime residents to "ranch the view," carrying with them a fantasy image of the West, didn't want the landscape messed up by those trying to earn a living in the place.

Environmentalists invoked arguments against cutting trees, scarring the countryside with roads, and fouling the water with sewage and erosion. Unfortunately, the power of their arguments was sometimes weakened by a few of their more vocal spokesmen, whose lavish homes and lifestyles (the glass-house syndrome) contrasted considerably with their environmental concerns. At least no yuppie backpackers or mountain bikers appeared to complain about cow pies on mountain trails, as happened in Telluride, Aspen, and Crested Butte. In fact, no one even suggested that the livestock industry should move or be replaced by tourism or any other activity.

Outside experts brought in by advocates of one position or the other were quickly dismissed by most observers as little more than hired guns. Ouray County residents had little use for experts; most viewed them as people who liked to create the problems they were later hired to solve. Experts from the Bureau of Reclamation or The Nature Conservancy appeared in the county from time to time to talk about dams, water use, and wildlife habitats, telling us we needed to conserve water or that riparian areas were being damaged by cattle (but not by elk or deer or buffalo). Cloud-seeding experts told local cattlemen in one snow-short winter in the late 1970s how they would "slightly modify" the weather to bring much-needed snow to a nearby ski area. Their efforts dumped record snows on Ridgway cattle and wildlife, resulting in higher feed bills for both local ranchers and the Colorado Division of Wildlife. Experts appeared on *Good Morning America* and told us and the rest of the country how to raise our children and what not to eat— like beef—because laboratory mice fed quarter-pounders died a terrible death. As most county residents recognized, experts made their living cooped up in university classrooms and laboratories and knew nothing about the real world or how to make a living off the land. In short, they were outsiders being paid immense sums to transmit misinformation, particularly on local land-use issues.

The old-timers, oddly enough, did not always share the antidevelopment sentiment. They carried with them the long-standing frontier belief that private property rights were inviolate and that any form of zoning for whatever public purpose was a threat to their Fifth Amendment guarantee that private property could not be taken without just compensation. At the same time, however, the old-timers did not want to see Ridgway turned into the personal playground of a bunch of trust-fund recreationists from Telluride and elsewhere.

Longtime residents did go out of their way to disagree with the hobby ranchers, not out of envy or even spite, but for what might be characterized as the I've-lived-here-longer-than-you-have argument. Their parents and grandparents had worked and suffered and persevered in their successful efforts to settle this country, and the children and grandchildren of the pioneers felt they were entitled to a louder voice than that given to the "damned newcomers," no matter how much money they had.

The main reason for disagreement, however, was strictly economic. If development had to occur, many old-time ranchers argued, then they—the legitimate landowners—wanted to profit, too. The newcomers in their expensive hillside houses wanted to preserve their vistas, but it was the working ranchers who paid the bills to maintain the open spaces. The best incentive for them not to sell their land for development, they said, was higher cattle prices. Until then, no one had the right to tell them what they could or couldn't do with their private property. "Tell me why I can't sell off a hillside to a developer where a prairie dog would starve to death, and I'll tell you why you should move your butt back to Texas," I heard one rancher exclaim at a land-use planning meeting.

The Ouray newspaper quoted a Texan whose plan for a forty-acre subdivision on his property outside Ridgway met strong opposition before the Planning Commission. "Local ranchers," he said, "need to understand that agriculture is dead in this county. They should all get on a bus and leave." In other words, the ranchers ought to sell out and move on, thankful for the small profit offered us by those willing (and able) to rejuvenate the county's sleepy economy. We wondered why we had to leave on buses rather than drive out in our pickups. And the Texan didn't even offer to pay our bus fare! What came through loud and clear, however, was the frustration of the Texan, and other speculators, with the many local residents who wanted to protect the county's beautiful landscape against speculative development.

After almost two years of public hearings, the county commissioners, on the recommendation of the Planning Commission, approved a compromise plan to allow higher density (clustered housing) in "recreational" developments within the foothill and alpine zones in exchange for the dedication of open space. In addition, strict visual impact restrictions were placed on all new buildings in all zones. The ski resort proposal died for lack of community support, but the Fairway Pines development on Log Hill utilized the new cluster regulation to expand.

Out-of-town developers and local land investors were not pleased with the new land-use regulations, many of which they attempted either to circumvent or to ignore. But once they recognized that the county intended to enforce the rules, they either looked to other Colorado counties for easier pickings or worked within the regulations to develop attractive and affordable new housing. To this day, nothing arouses the local citizenry more than an attempt (legal or extralegal) to amend or circumvent the county's land-use regulations. The rules are constantly reviewed, and pragmatically refined, to maintain a peaceful and equitable balance between those who wish to halt all development and those who would happily cover the landscape with mobile home parks and put a 7-Eleven at each intersection.

Flouting the efforts of Ouray County officials to discourage strip-town development along the valley floor, especially along U.S. 550, the main highway that bisects the county from north to south, the town of Ridgway encouraged such development. As an incorporated town, Ridgway had the authority to establish its own land-use regulations independent of the county's codes. Shortly after the county approved its slow-growth plan, Ridgway's political dynamics dictated major development to satisfy the growing demand for jobs and an increased tax base. To the consternation of many county residents, Ridgway town officials approved plans for Ridgway USA, which included a new motel and a tourist attraction called Trail Town, a series of stores and small shops to be located along U.S. 550. Probably more than any other institution or development project in the county, Trail Town symbolized the cultural conflict between old-time agriculturalists and commerce-minded newcomers.

Ridgway's Trail Town portrays Ridgway as a wild gunslinging cattle town instead of a more peaceful railroad stop. The misrepresentation plays to the frontier myths of the Old West, popular with tourists to the area. Courtesy of Otto Scheidegger

Trail Town plays to the old Hollywood vision of the romantic West—cowboys, cattle, and Comanches. Visitors enter shops designed to confirm the West, past and present, as a gigantic cattle kingdom filled with romantic cowboys who, when not riding the sagebrush or sitting around a campfire singing "Home on the Range," shoot down bad guys and rye whiskey—usually simultaneously. That Ridgway was a community of farmers, dairymen, ranchers, and freighters serving the mines, not a cow town like Cheyenne, Ogallala, or Dodge City, seems never to have occurred to Trail Town's creators—or if it did was ignored because an accurate history of the area did not conform to their roman-tic image. In short, Trail Town as it attempts to transform Ridgway into a theme park mutilates and sells short what it pretends to elevate and embrace. Its shops sell cowboy boots, of course; not the plain, stiff-leather type made for riding or mucking through manure, but designer boots in supple patent leather created for the dance floor that disintegrate at the first contact with dirt or water. Cowboy hats come in purple and lime green, and the cut of the designer jeans the shops sell makes it dif-ficult to mount a horse.

Adjacent to Trail Town is The Big Barn, a creation of Dennis Weaver, former star of the television series *Gunsmoke*. On summer weekends, tourists fill this big dance hall, where a country-western band provides Ridgway's only live music. They love the "western" atmosphere, especially the decorative cowboys saddled up to the bar, who look like objects out of a Roy Rogers movie. When I didn't recog-nize two of the cowboys at the bar and asked a friend who they were, he identified them as "rental cowboys" brought in to add a little atmos-phere. They sure looked the part: men with rough, chiseled faces and the appropriate long handlebar mustaches swigging from long-necked Coors bottles; faded jeans tucked into their high-top boots, attached to which were dangling spurs; big high-crowned Tom Mix hats; and long duster jackets with just the right amount of dirt to hint of a hard day's drive out on the range. They never managed to get out on the dance floor—hindered, perhaps, by those spurs—but remained locked to the bar rail as they drawled out yarns to the fawning tourists. I gave their hands a good look but didn't detect any calluses.

Another group of local "cowboys" in Trail Town offers an educational experience to passing tourists in a presentation entitled "Legends of the West." These men, with their "intense commitment to research history," guarantee visitors a "faithful" portrayal of "the gentle school marm, the dance hall girls, and the proud pioneer women who raised families in the West." "The gunmen of the West," tourists are informed, "became outlaws because they were persecuted." This little history lesson of how hardworking, God-fearing, upstanding citizens were transformed into cold-blooded murderers is presented every evening for $8 (discounted for senior citizens) in the form of a hanging and shoot-out. Business is brisk, and the "Legends" are so popular that they perform at events throughout the region.

Next door, tourists interested in learning more about "Native American traditions" are educated by the "Memory Makers," who know all about the "crusty hard men, toughened to the rough life ... as savage as the Indians with whom they lived." With everyone seated around a campfire, a contemporary mountain man shares his historical wisdom about fur trapping and trading beads while demonstrating for the tourists how to throw a tomahawk at a wooden stump from thirty paces. A tourist may enhance this educational experience by spending the night in an "authentic" Indian tepee. And to ensure the tourist's comfort, the Memory Makers have placed a sign outside the tepee to indicate the location of the nearest portable potty (across the lane, adjacent to the Motel 8 swimming pool).

The offerings at Trail Town are good clean fun and provide inexpensive and convenient entertainment, and maybe, for some, an educational experience. And what's the matter with a theme park that brings business to town, argue Trail Town's defenders. Disneyland does it, and so does the Buffalo Bill Museum in Cody, Wyoming—granted, on a different scale and with a bit more élan, but there are thousands of similar tourist traps placed across the western landscape to fleece visitors of their dollars. The Black Hills are dotted with "Olde" military forts, tepee villages, and trading posts. You can buy "authentic" six-shooters, T-shirts, and rubber tomahawks on every corner in Jackson, Wyoming. Museums in small towns and major cities depict the story of the brave homesteaders and tough cowboys who tamed a rough frontier wilderness of brutish Indians and nasty gunfighters and brought law and order to a young community of honest, hardworking Christians.

The old-timers of Ouray County are quick to tell you, however, that Trail Town is something less than an educational experience. "It is an abomination, that's what it is," one rancher complained to me. In its attempt to portray the county's history for the tourists, Trail Town has trivialized that history beyond recognition and, worse, has insulted the older generation of pioneer sons and daughters, who know the county's history to be far different from the stereotyped invention created at Trail Town. Forget the Italian miners, Scandinavian dairymen, Eastern European grain farmers, Basque sheepherders, Chinese rail builders, German train crews, female shopkeepers, widows, and teenage runaways who worked in the town. Remember only a romantic fantasy of mountain men, Indians, cowboys, and gunmen created in Hollywood and transported to Ridgway. Remain silent about how Anglo greed traded away the Ute Indians for gold and silver; ignore the absence of gunmen; and for fear of tarnishing the romantic image of the place, for heaven's sake don't mention the massive failure of the homesteaders in the early decades of this century. In their cynical reinvention of history designed to engender nostalgia for a past that never was, these fantasy-making commercial hucksters in their tiny theme park genuinely believe they provide a positive contribution to the town's welfare and an educational experience for tourists.

Supporting their argument, not surprisingly, is the local Chamber of Commerce. With its gunmen, mountain men, and shopkeepers, Trail

Town has created jobs for residents. Tourists spend their money in local restaurants and shops, and by doing so prime the pump of the local economy. The Trail Town shops pay town and county taxes, which help to pay for the public services demanded by residents new and old. And don't forget, the Chamber of Commerce is quick to remind critics, the real estate sales Trail Town generates both in its own sales office and at other burgeoning real estate offices in town. The real estate brokers, supported by the Chamber of Commerce, like to point out that it is they who are responsible for the growth that has come to Ridgway, they who have provided ranchers with a very profitable market for their largest resource—land. The local rancher cashes out with a hefty profit, the real estate folks get their commissions, and the county has acquired a new taxpayer. "It's a win-win situation," the chamber brags to anyone willing to listen.

—————•••—————

Along with growth in the mid-1980s and 1990s came increasing demands for better services, including roads, police and fire protection, and social services. Ridgway had to hire an extra police deputy, and the county sheriff's department added four new deputies when petty crime (mostly theft) and domestic violence increased throughout the county. And, of course, taxes had to be raised to pay for the added services. The county commissioners were continually bombarded with requests to improve the muddy, rough dirt roads and crumbling bridges that once served only outlying ranches but are now thoroughfares to housing developments.

And what was the city to do with all the garbage generated by a population that had almost doubled in two decades? "Not in my back-yard," was the refrain at public meetings. Clearly the old garbage pit just up the hill west of Ridgway was no longer adequate. It was a great place for town kids to improve their shooting skills on the increasing rat population, but the smoke and odor of burning garbage violated

Ridgway's new image of itself as a tourist destination. The commissioners moved the dump (later sanitized to a "landfill," then euphemized
further to become a "waste management transfer station") to the east
side of town in 1976. It sits today on a plot overlooking the town with
a panoramic view of the San Juan Mountains, surely one of the nation's
most spectacular settings for a landfill. Gone are the fires burning last
month's garbage or an old mattress. Gone too are the days when the
old dump served as something of a community swap shop, where it
was possible to leave a legless sofa and pick up in return an outdated,
but still usable, refrigerator.

But of all the issues that caused internal conflicts within Ouray
County, the direction of Ridgway's only public school (K–12) generated
the most heated and angry debates. The school became the lightning rod
that provided the forum for conflict not so much between generations
as between "traditional" values and "foreign" values imported into the
county by new residents. For generations, the school had served as the
cultural preserve of families born and raised in the county. The sons and
daughters of ranchers, craftsmen, and shopkeepers were taught the value
of discipline and hard work, and the skills necessary to work alongside
their parents and grandparents after graduation.

The school offered an appropriate education for its time, despite
its rather parochial and insular focus. But when the economics of ranching
changed in the late 1960s and early 1970s, and ranches could no longer
support two, much less three, generations, the children of ranchers had
to leave the county in search of other employment. And what was true
for ranch children was also true for the sons and daughters of local
craftsmen, miners, and shopkeepers. Job opportunities in the county
were limited. Residents realized that they had to prepare and educate
their children for a different, and larger, world.

Most county residents agreed that the school's overcrowded physical
plant needed to be expanded, and the discussions about how to finance
the improvements were fairly mild. The acrimony started when it came

time to decide how to educate the students and what to teach them. Many old-time residents refused to recognize that their children needed skills not taught to them a generation earlier when they attended Ridgway's school. Parents who had finished Ridgway High School and gone to work or war during the 1930s and early 1940s saw no reason why their children needed the luxury of a college education; certainly it was not a prerequisite for ranching. There was also the recognition, if not the fear, that college-educated children, particularly sons, might be attracted to the outside world, away from the ranch. If it was good enough for me, parents said to their children, it's good enough for you. The school mirrored these standards well into the 1970s, when, not surprisingly, the state and the school board fought over certification standards.

Despite the changing job market in the 1970s and 1980s and the availability of affordable state colleges nearby, some parents continued to argue against a precollege curriculum that included competence in a foreign language, four years of English, three years of mathematics (including algebra and geometry), and a basic knowledge of American history and government. Such a curriculum was designed only for the few students who wanted to go on to college, said these parents; "elitist" courses should not be allowed to replace home economics, bookkeeping, study methods, auto mechanics, and Colorado history. And they were outraged when the newcomers wanted to cut athletic programs to balance the school's budget. Only in the 1990s, after many furious and heated debates, did the academic standards improve to the point that a student today can obtain an education that prepares him or her for entrance into one of the state's many institutions of higher education.

The school board, no longer composed of an older, agricultural generation, is now controlled by parents born outside the county. It is the preserve of fundamentalist Christians, relative newcomers to Ridgway, whose religious beliefs are reflected in the educational policies and operation of the school, including, critics claim, the selection and promotion of faculty and staff. Defenders of the school and its board, claiming to

be the inheritors of "traditional values," claim there is now a more structured and disciplined learning atmosphere, where drugs and alcohol (a
growing problem in the county) are no longer tolerated. Some critics
complain the school is administered like a quasi-military boot camp where
intolerance for new ideas is the major impediment to a high-quality
education. In the Ridgway school, as in schools across the nation, it is the
age-old debate: what to teach and how to teach it. Why isn't sex education taught? Why must a lock-step grade system be so rigidly designed
around the common denominator of the "average" student when there
are students (fast and slow learners) who require a more flexible learning
environment? Despite the controversy and the school's limited resources,
however, the school does provide an environment for small-class learning, and particularly in the lower grades, some extraordinary teachers.

The school continues to be the lightning rod for conflicting interests and values within the Ridgway area. The one constant is the lack
of jobs for those graduates who wish to remain, work, and live where
they went to school. Like nearly every rural area in the nation, Ridgway
continues to export its most valuable commodity—its youth. The new
highly mechanized ranches offer few jobs. Following the national trend,
the number of agricultural workers in the county has declined by more
than 50 percent in the last thirty years. And the jobs available in Ridgway, Ouray, and Telluride tend increasingly to be in the service sector,
waiting tables, cleaning motel rooms, driving a van, or attending a
chairlift. The armed forces attract some graduates, as do trade schools.
But almost all graduates, including those who finish college or university, must look for jobs in cities far distant from their home.

More than half of Ridgway High's graduates now go on to complete college, a far higher percentage than twenty years ago. Unfortunately, there continues to exist in the Ridgway school, as in most public
schools across the country, a culture among students in which medioc-
rity defines the norm. Any talented teenager must hide his or her intel-
lectual interests for fear of peer ridicule. And as in most schools across

the country, the authorities are too quick to blame kids (and their parents) for disciplinary problems when the real problem may be boredom caused by the lack of academic challenges. But the school is the single institution that represents the town, and citizens take pride in its graduates and championship athletic teams. If, as suggested by most residents, the high school were to be combined with the school in Ouray, Ridgway would lose much of its self-identity and sense of community.

———

Ridgway often brags that it is a community—a town whose citizens share common values and obligations. But the generation who came of age in the 1930s, survivors of the Depression born to hard work on the county's ranches and mines, share neither similar backgrounds nor values with most of the new residents. Among the post-Depression generation, those brought up to believe that one advances in life through rugged individualism, the older habits of cooperation have weakened. There is little recognition, as Barry Lopez has suggested in *The Rediscovery of North America*, of the difference "between the kind of independence that is a desire to be responsible to no one but the self—the independence of the adolescent—and the independence that means the assumption of responsibility in society, the independence of people who no longer need to be supervised." The self-congratulatory bragging one hears from some of the newer Ridgway residents—how rugged they are, how they acquired what they own through hard work and individual effort—rarely mentions any cooperative enterprise. Their achievements have been attained, I suspect, at great cost to any notion of a larger community obligation and the maintenance of the delicate balance between individualism and social justice. Such is the nature of late-twentieth-century communities.

A Different Town in a New West

Talk at the Ridgway coffee shop had revolved around cattle prices and
the weather for as long as I could remember. Ranchers whose livelihood
depended on calf prices at the weekly cattle auction in Montrose and
timely rains through the summer months were far more concerned about
weather patterns off the coast of California and Mexico than they were
with the direction of the Dow Jones average or who won a presidential
debate. By the early 1990s, however, the general subjects of conversation
in the coffee shop had changed.

Tourists filled the shop all summer, asking locals where to fish, what
jeep trails were open in the mountains, how to get to Telluride, and the
average price of a local house lot. An increasing number of new residents filed into the post office each morning to pick up their mail. The
old-timers complained about the newcomers, said they didn't recognize
anyone at the post office anymore, and talked about the damned hunter
from Texas who mistook a pack horse over near the OXO Ranch for a
bull elk.

"Remember when" stories became very popular. Like the story of
old Jim Harrison, a six-foot-four mule skinner who ran a small herd
of cattle on his homestead at the head of Beaver Creek when he wasn't
hauling ore from the mines. In the midst of the Depression, Jim's cattle
loan came due at the Ridgway bank. After trailing cattle into Ridgway

from his ranch some eight miles away in early November, he walked into the office of the bank president, Mr. Walther, and asked for an extension of his loan until spring. "Can't do that, Jim," Mr. Walter said. Looking out the bank window at his cattle in the street, Jim responded: "Well, there are your cattle. You feed 'em." Jim got his loan extension, and Marie Scott helped him with the payoff by buying his homestead; she continued to look after Jim until he died in the 1960s.

By the 1990s, cattle ranching no longer defined the local economy. Where in 1975 some nineteen thousand head of cattle were raised in the county, twenty years later there were fewer than six thousand. Ranchers realized that their meadows and pastures were valuable homesites, too valuable, perhaps, for grazing cows. Some of those who continued ranching on their high-priced real estate owned their land free and clear or owed only a small mortgage, and some possessed considerable off-ranch income that allowed them the luxury of not having to worry about making a profit from their livestock. The many ranchers in the area, including myself, who fell into neither category began seriously thinking about moving our livestock operations out of Ridgway and into areas where the cost of land and labor better matched the economics of the cattle business.

It didn't require a banker or an economist with a Ph.D. to understand that if a cow needed approximately three acres of irrigated meadow (with a 1996 market value of approximately $4,000 per acre) for herself and her calf for a year, and if the value of the weaned calf in the best of times was $500, the return on the rancher's investment was 4 percent *before* subtracting expenses. One rancher told me, "Heck, I'd double my income this year and probably for the foreseeable future if I sold off my herd and land, paid the taxes, retired my debt, and invested the remainder in Treasury bills." Unless one married into or inherited a ranch large enough to support a family and generate a profit (a very unlikely scenario, given inheritance taxes), it made little economic sense by the 1990s to buy expensive land in the Ridgway area for a livestock operation, or even to continue ranching when the incentives to sell were so enticing.

The simply equation for the production of cattle is basically the same as it is for cars or computers: the larger the operation, the lower the per-unit cost of production and the higher the profit margin. But the high land prices around Ridgway prevented ranchers from expanding to a profitable size. The average land cost for running one cow unit (cow and calf) in the Rocky Mountain West in 1993 was somewhere between $2,500 and $4,000, but the value of Ridgway land had escalated the cow unit land cost there to $12,000! In the span of two decades, the price of a Ridgway ranch with a view of the mountains had increased four times, yet the income from a cow had increased, at most, only about 30 percent. And irrigation water, the lifeblood of the land, now commanded three times its agricultural value in commercial sales locally and immediately downstream toward Montrose.

Grazing cattle in the shadow of the San Juan Mountains. Ranching History of Ouray County of the Ridgway Public Library

It made little economic sense for me to continue to run cattle on land that had increased far beyond its agricultural value when I wanted to expand my livestock herd. In addition, my operating costs (transportation, feed, equipment, and labor) continued to increase. Local hourly wage standards were set not by the economics of the cattle industry but by what construction crews were paying in Telluride. Itinerant cowboys came through with a pickup and a saddle looking for summer employment, but it didn't take a long interview to understand that most of them were all hat and no skill. The young men with good ranch skills preferred to pound nails for $15 an hour rather than fix fences or check calves in a blizzard for $5. The agricultural economy simply could not compete with the recreational economy.

Rather than fight the recreational economy—and to help cover their rising labor costs—a few local ranchers joined it and began taking in tourists seeking a *City Slicker* experience. Vacationers from New York, Los Angeles, and Cleveland got to play cowboy while working on roundups, brandings, and other ranch chores. Cowboys and cowgirls from New Jersey loved trailing cattle in the mountains or chasing a renegade steer across a meadow, although I never heard of any who enjoyed fixing fences and digging postholes on a hot summer day. One local rancher in Ridgway who used guests on his hay crew, and urged me to do the same, said of his dudes: "If they're dumb enough to want to do it and *pay* for it, I'm smart enough to let them do it and take their money." I tried using the teenage sons and daughters of city friends and relatives on the ranch, but with a couple of exceptions, what I saved in labors costs I more than gave up in repair bills and supervisory time. In the end, for me and for others, there was no way around the high costs of the Ridgway area.

The idea of selling my ranch and moving to an area with lower production costs looked even more attractive to me when I realized that cattle prices, like almost all agricultural commodities (wheat, corn, pork bellies), have not kept pace with prices in the larger general economy.

To put it simply, agricultural production in the United States continues to outpace rising demand, even if foreign markets are included. A ranch woman from a nearby town reminded me not long ago of a critical lesson in agricultural economics. "Why is it," she asked me, "that in the 1950s it took the proceeds from the sale of ten calves to buy a pickup. Today, it takes fifty critters to buy a truck ... and another three if I want four-wheel drive." I had no immediate answer for her, but I did recognize that if I wanted to keep on raising cattle, I'd have to continue to cut my per unit cost of production. The best way to accomplish that was to run more cows with essentially the same overhead (labor and equipment) costs on inexpensive yet productive land. When I asked my foreman for his opinion, he responded: "It's difficult to work around here when more and more people want to recreate. Cattle are raised by a work ethic, not the play ethic."

I had to agree, especially after a hot-air balloon loaded with tourists appeared over our corrals on Saturday morning in early May just as the branding was getting under way. The large yellow-and-orange monster in the sky with its hissing air heater scared five hundred cows and an equal number of calves out of separate holding pens and halfway to Kansas. After the four hours it took us to recapture the cattle and resort the cows and the calves, it was too hot to further stress the calves. We put off the branding to the next day—when, of course, it rained. I swore at the balloonists just as I swore at the tourists who left the gates open on our summer range, and those who had snowmobiled through our cattle the previous winter. Besides the increasing problems with trespassers, my ranch accounts with a few exceptions reflected losses even in the good years when cattle prices were high. As for the cows, they didn't take to the increasing number of skiers, snowmobilers, dogs, and fences. They couldn't eat snow, and they sure as hell didn't ski.

My family's decision to move was by no means shared by a majority of the county ranchers. Some contemplated selling out and retiring to town, and a few of the older ones did so. But the decision to sell, to see land that had been in a family for three or even four generations turned into cash, was difficult despite the high prices offered. When I asked my neighbor Denise Adams, whose family has been ranching continuously in the Ridgway-Telluride area for the last eighty years, if she ever though about selling out, she said no without hesitation. "This is home ... you don't sell it. You sell off your land and what have you got? Some cash. But look what you've lost: your inheritance." For Denise, it was an unequal exchange at any price. Ranching is a way of life. You ranch for the love of it, and aside from the economics of the enterprise, you never go broke—although your banker might disagree and force a foreclosure.

Ranchers who contemplated exchanging one ranch for another discovered other areas in the West where land, water, feed, and labor were not only cheaper but also more readily available—especially labor. Not surprisingly, these areas were far distant from the recreational centers in the spectacular mountain valleys of the Rockies. Ranchers throughout western Colorado, northwestern Wyoming, and even parts of southwestern Montana, pressured by the second-home recreational economy, sought new beginnings in the flat eastern plains of Montana, Wyoming, and Colorado. We joined that migration in 1993 when we sold off more than half our ranch, including most of the productive hay meadows, and moved the equipment, cattle, ranch manager, and his family to the lush grasslands of the Nebraska Sandhills. We held on to our home and some surrounding acreage west of Ridgway, which we leased to our neighbors.

The business decision to relocate our cattle operation more than five hundred miles away in Nebraska was relatively simple; far more difficult for my family and me was the emotional dislocation involved in separating ourselves from land on which we had earned a livelihood for many years. You get attached to a piece of land not so much because you own it as because you've put so much energy into making it productive.

Selling my favorite meadow—the one just north of the corrals at the Dry Creek ranch—was like saying good-bye to a close relative I knew I'd never see again. Over the years I had come to know every shallow swale and high ridge along its backbone. I had picked rocks off its smooth face, leaving pockmarks that soon filled with silt, and I had watered it lovingly like a flower every summer. In return, it produced a magnificent crop of timothy, brome, and orchard grass. Its hay was always the lushest on the ranch. When haying it, I had to gear the swather down into second in order to move smoothly through the waist-high grass and not stall out. The cows, too, appreciated this meadow. It was the first one they grazed after being brought down from the mountains in the fall, and they devoured its baled hay in the winter as if it were spiked with sugar and molasses.

Close by on the lower end of the Dry Creek ranch, which was defined by a deep drainage ditch paid for by one of President Roosevelt's farm programs in the 1930s, coyotes constantly prowled the high ditch bank, looking for the prairie dogs that burrowed into its side. One coyote with a distinctive slit in its ear visited me every summer in the lower Sneva meadow as I circled with the hay rake. It would trot along behind me and, as the rake turned over the hay and uncovered field mice, feast on the harvest. Although I never saw him in the winter, we became good summer friends. The coyote never bothered the cattle, at least not that I was aware of, and it came every summer morning during the haying season to accompany me on my rounds through the hay fields.

The adjoining meadow had its problems, and I wasn't too sorry to let someone else take on those headaches. Its steep slope and thin soils gave me trouble from the day I made my first irrigation set there. I tried for years without success to heal two deep cuts in that meadow, and I left more sweat, broken shovel handles, and expletives there than any other place on the ranch. In addition, the son-of-a-bitch culvert under the road that ran to the field never failed to wash out every spring, even though I reset it every summer in a new bed of gravel braced with large rocks.

Nevertheless, I miss the meadows and the rutted dirt road that serves it. Late each spring, as I approached this meadow to make my first water set of the irrigation season, I'd be greeted by thirty or so killdeer, their black breast bands and white wing stripes flashing, crying their loud, plaintive warning. "Dee-dee-dee," they'd scream as one female faked a broken wing to lure me away from her nest in the tall grass close to the road. The cows would miss the thick stand of cedars on the meadow's northern edge that in one horrible April blizzard in 1983 provided life-giving shelter to a small group of young heifers and their newborn calves. From this same spot I watched two bald eagles make their winter headquarters for seven years. The winter we moved, they did not return.

I knew I would miss Buckingham Palace and the grove of trees around it, too. The Palace, the old Brandt homestead cabin, hadn't seen a repair since Otto Brandt's widow sold it to Juan Pouchoulou in the 1920s. Juan, a Basque immigrant who started off in this country as a sheepherder near Montrose, put together a good-sized sheep outfit of his own and used the Brandt cabin to house his herders before he sold his sheep and land in 1975 and retired to France. When we bought the Pouchoulou Ranch, cattle had been camping out in the cabin's living room and kitchen, and one bovine had even made it up the steep stairs to the bedroom, where it had left its calling cards. We let young work-men such as Tom McKenney, who couldn't locate affordable housing in town, stay in the cabin in return for making some repairs and improvements. When we sold the property in 1993, Buckingham Palace, with its repaired roof and porch, sanded floors, painted interior, and Rube Goldberg plumbing, was once again a comfortable cabin in a spectacular setting.

Our cows liked to calve in the thick grove of juniper trees that sur-rounded that cabin. Early one Sunday morning, in the midst of a horrible March storm, my daughter Hilary (then eight) and I were driving by the cabin when we noticed a cow lying beneath a tree. We stopped the truck and walked up to see if the cow was having difficulty calving, and clearly she was. The calf's front legs were out, and I could just see the top of its head, but the cow was exhausted and had all but given up pushing. I went back to my truck and got a rope, threw it around the cow's neck, and snubbed her close to a tree. She immediately fell on her side and soon tried again to push out the calf, but made no progress. I stretched myself out on the cow's flank to keep her on her side and then told Hilary to pull on the calf's legs from the rear. "The calf is going to die," she sobbed. "If you don't pull hard on those feet, she will," I responded with some irritation, "so set your feet against the cow's rump and keep pulling those legs HARD." Sitting in about a foot of snow in her bulky snowsuit, she pulled on the calf's slippery legs with all the strength an eight-year-old ranch girl could muster. The calf popped out like a cork from a bottle onto my daughter's chest, along with quarts of bloody afterbirth. Tears ran down her face—not, I quickly learned, of fear or horror, but for the total pleasure of having saved a life. It was a wonderful moment shared in a grove of trees we were both going to miss.

Deedee and I would miss working alongside some of our neighbors, like Ray Hutt, who could bring humor to the coldest, meanest day. We'd no longer attend the midwinter gathering of the Ouray Cattlemen's Association in the old Cow Creek community hall, where on a subzero February evening we'd huddle together in the uninsulated building over a steak and green Jell-O salad, gathering warmth from those in attendance, including Jim Beam.

And like our livestock, we would miss even such mundane things as the corrals. We appreciated them not because we built them over a period of ten years, hand-digging and blasting the postholes into unforgiving shale and skillfully notching and wiring the rails to the posts, but because the cattle were so familiar with the interior design that once inside the maze of alleys, pens, and gates, they knew exactly where to go. In Nebraska, the livestock would have to learn a new corral design in addition to where to hide from the prevailing winter winds, the location of water, the best grasses, and how to work around and through unfamiliar pastures and gates.

I left behind my two work horses, Howard and Hershel, who had grown to maturity on the ranch. Nebraska, I knew, would not suit them. There would be no deep snow there, and no need for them to pull a hay sled every winter morning, so I gave them to Mario Zadra, a local rancher. Mario, who as a young man hauled ore out of the Camp Bird mine with a sixteen-mule team in the 1930s, and who had taught me how to train and drive a team, would, I knew, appreciate and take care of Howard and Hershel. I knew I would miss seeing them rush into the horse barn for their early morning meal of grain before being led outside to be harnessed. They always assisted me when I put on their collars, dipping their heads in unison as if to say, "Good morning, Pete." Hershel would nip playfully at my back pocket, wanting to get another lick of snuff, while Howard, the calm, serious one and the heavy puller of the team, waited impatiently for me to throw the harness over his broad, muscular back. When I had them fully harnessed and ready to go to work, without a word or a lead they would immediately walk over to the wagon, Howard always on the left and Hershel on the right, and back themselves gently toward the doubletree where the harness tugs attached to the wagon, taking care not to step on the wagon tongue. When they heard the sound of the tug's links connecting to the doubletree, Howard and Hershel would lift their heads and playfully do a little jig as if to say, "We're ready for work, boss, so let's get after it. The quicker we get finished feeding the cows, the sooner we'll be back here for another bucket of grain."

We knew we would miss two old barns, too. One had served as the milk barn for Mr. Sneva, who homesteaded the property in the 1880s. We had removed the primitive wooden stanchions and redesigned the space to make room for horse stalls and a place to saddle up out of the winter wind. We replaced the worn-out wooden floors with thick cottonwood planks, and the old shake roof with a metal one; some of the leather window straps had rotted and had to be replaced. But other than those small repairs, the barn was pretty much as Mr. Sneva had built it a hundred years ago. I wouldn't miss the expense of annual repairs to Mr. Sneva's ditch, which started on Cow Creek, six miles to the south, and traversed neighboring ranches on its way to our ranch; but I would remember fondly the Sneva meadows where I could make an irrigation set, allow the water to seep slowly across the flat landscape, and not worry about it for a week.

Of all the things that made the move to the Nebraska Sandhills so very difficult for me, however, perhaps the most important was recognizing that the spectacularly beautiful and productive Colorado land I was selling might be carved up into housing tracts, a golf course, or, as one prospective buyer had suggested, a cemetery. A Texas scam artist visited my ranch and offered to give me full partnership in the Rocky Mountain Cemetery in return for my donating 860 acres to this exciting and profitable enterprise. By his reckoning, we could plant sixty-four folks to the acre and still have space left over for a chapel, walking paths, and RV campsites for overnight guests. He assured me we'd make a hell of a profit. How he reached his scientific body count, I had no idea; but I did know I wasn't excited about becoming a mortician. I declined the partnership opportunity but continued to worry that the new owner of our property would trash one of America's most beautiful valleys.

As it turned out, I worried needlessly. I had failed to recognize that the high per-acre price of my large parcel (more than half of which was irrigated meadows) reduced the prospective field of buyers, including developers, who were limited by the zoning restrictions as to how many housing units they could build on the property. Other than the cemetery entrepreneur, those who inquired about my ranch, to my surprise, were either wealthy would-be ranchers looking to start a cattle operation in Ridgway or established ranchers looking to expand.

My ranch was "saved" the way other large parcels of land in and around Ridgway have been preserved—with money earned by a nonrancher outside the county. In the same way, and for many of the same reasons, that the ranches of Marie Scott, Harry McClure, and the Ethridge family changed hands without being split up and subdivided, my meadows and grazing ground along Dry Creek became home to a different set of cows and a new owner. The Texas doctor who purchased my ranch was smart enough to recognize that the price he paid could in no way be returned to him by record hay crops or even a doubling of cattle prices. Like so many other new landowners in the area, he bought the ranch for its beauty, its privacy, and the lifestyle it represented to him. In addition, of course, he recognized the importance of land as a hedge against inflation and the tax benefits of writing off ranch operating expenses against his nonranch (medical) income.

The traditional ranchers and older residents in the county have been quick to criticize the part-time summer ranchers, with their trophy homes, private jets, fancy horses, luxurious landscaping, and IRS cattle. And these people do make easy targets. Their style of ranching is, to put it gently, nontraditional. The brandings and roundups are exclusive affairs, complete with dance bands and catered meals, for out-of-town celebrities who want to play cowboy for a weekend. They don't share in the local tradition of neighboring—the brandings, the roundup, haying, etc.—for fear that a neighbor might be injured and might sue them. For the same reason their property is off-limits to locals who want to hunt, snowmobile, or fish.

Recently, a multimillionaire rancher in the Wet Mountain area of Colorado, an Australian who made his fortune manufacturing hair shampoo, asked all the guests at his wedding ("hitchin' party") to sign a waiver of any and all claims (deaths, injuries, illness, or damages) against him. As reported in the *Denver Post* (June 16, 1996), the weekend-long wedding festivities included trail rides, stagecoach rides, and a rodeo on the fifty-five-thousand-acre ranch stocked with cattle and 370 not-so-friendly buffalo. The *Wedding Gazette* that was sent to all invitees explained: "In the old West, justice used to be handed out by hanging parties and hot lead. Nowadays, we use lawyers and [they] say that we need to have you sign the enclosed release form if you're planning to attend." Although there was no hospital within miles of the ranch, the guests were no doubt comforted to read in the *Gazette* that four M.D.s would be attending as guests and that an ambulance and paramedics would be standing by eighteen hours a day.

Old-time ranchers like Marie Scott built for themselves modest structures (right). The modern ranchers who have moved into Ridgway prefer more pretentious "ranch homes," recently referred to by *The Wall Street Journal* as "starter castles."
Courtesy of Otto Scheidegger

And then there is the Californian who built a private chapel on his Ridgway ranch for his daughter's wedding. The same man is currently constructing a residential compound—complete with indoor shooting range and guest and staff quarters—that will exceed sixty thousand square feet and cost an estimated $30 million, almost three times the original price of the Louisiana Purchase. This Ridgway summer house is just another example of what the *Wall Street Journal* recently referred to as "starter castles." When I commented to a local artisan who works at the construction site that the pioneer generation of ranchers and their families from the entire Cow Creek area could fit comfortably into one of the structure's three floors, he responded: "You bet. You pass through two time zones going from the kitchen to the master bedroom suite [3,000 square feet]." The same ranch had Glen Campbell sing at their spring branding gathering.

These private preserves with their locked *Bonanza* gates (huge edifices constructed of gigantic logs, proudly described to me by one owner as an entrance with "balls") and perimeter fences are posted with signs that read "Keep Out" and "Private Property." Where I cross-country skied atop Dallas Divide on my first visit to Ouray County in the early 1970s, trespassers today are prosecuted. Even the employees on these ranches—cooks, pilots, gardeners, housekeepers, mechanics, and cowboys—rarely receive permission to hunt or fish.

"I don't know if some of these people will ever be totally accepted by the community," Reeves Brown, executive director of the Colorado Cattlemen's Association, was quoted in a *Denver Post* article. "When your livelihood depends on your ability to work with the land and work with the community, and be a neighbor, you look different at someone who does it for fun."

Yet for all the criticism leveled against them and their "cowboy playgrounds," the hobby ranchers have had a positive influence. "We generate a tremendous amount of economic activity in this area," said John Ivory, manager of the ten-thousand-acre Sleeping Indian Ranch in

Ridgway, in the same *Denver Post* article. First, they have preserved ranching as one of the major economic activities in the county. When Ralph Lauren's Double RL Ranch began major construction projects (houses, barns, shops, corrals, etc.) in the 1980s, it was the largest employer in the county. In addition to basic construction requirements, the Double RL and ranches like it have provided employment to local artisans (e.g., stonemasons and cabinet and stained-glass makers) whose skills might otherwise go unrecognized in less expensive buildings. Lauren has donated to the Ridgway school a satellite system that allows students to enroll in precollege courses. Another absentee rancher has donated to the Ouray and Ridgway high schools a very substantial college scholarship fund for graduating seniors. And although they pay a large percentage of the county's taxes, these ranchers neither demand nor receive their fair share of benefits in return.

Most important, the very existence of these huge ranches has preserved close to 80,000 acres of open land—almost half the private land in the county. Wildlife habitats remain intact; the housing developments and mobile home parks that are so prevalent in Montrose County to the north do not clutter the lush grass valleys; and the hay meadows remain, as much for the benefit of their owners as for that of neighbors and tourists who similarly appreciate the open landscape. The wealth of the new landowners allows them to preserve and maintain a pastoral beauty, if not an Arcadian idyll, that the vast majority of county residents and visitors find very attractive. The work Ralph Lauren and others have done to preserve Ridgway has been replicated by other wealthy individuals throughout the Rocky Mountain West.

Some ranchers, particularly those who derive income from their ranches, use conservation easements, an arrangement that protects their land from development in perpetuity. In return for placing a permanent conservation easement on all or part of his or her property, the rancher receives a charitable income-tax deduction based on the appraised value of the donated development rights (the difference between a property's value if it were sold for a subdivision and its agricultural value). The rancher continues to own and operate the ranch, and the land trust, the recipient of the conservation easement, ensures that the ranch property is preserved and maintained in the condition agreed to by the current owner and all subsequent owners.

There are now land trusts in every western state with open land. The trusts, such as the Colorado Cattlemen's Agricultural Land Trust and the Colorado Conservation Trust, receive and administer conservation easements, purchase development rights with private money, and advise ranchers on estate management strategies. So far their efforts have met with considerable success, inspite of the sheer scope and power of the national and regional economies that wish to subdivide and dismantle open space, particularly agricultural land. In the Rocky Mountain region, the acreage and tax deductions involved are particularly large because of escalating land values, mounting development pressures, and the sheer size of the parcels being protected. In Colorado, the number of acres protected by land trusts doubled to close to 350,000 acres in the last three years. The influx of wealthy ranch buyers accounted for a majority of the acreage protected by state and national land trusts.

For traditional ranchers with little or no income except for that which they derive from their cattle, the charitable income-tax deduction received from the donation of a conservation easement is of no use because there is little income against which to offset the donation. The easement concept, while it protects land from development, does not always provide what many ranchers need most to survive—hard cash.

A land conservation organization in Gunnison, Colorado, plans to purchase development rights from ranchers. Most of the cash used to buy the rights comes from Great Outdoors Colorado (GOCO), a state agency that receives its funds from the tax proceeds of the state lottery. The state funds are supplemented with cash generated by a small Gunnison County sales tax, federal funds from the Farmland Protection Act, and some private money, primarily from local businesses. The cash received by the rancher for the development rights can be invested in an annuity and the annual income put toward the continued operation of the ranch. Although still in its infancy, the program has saved some ranches from subdivision and is, in addition to zoning, another tool currently used to preserve open space and ranchland.

Many ranchers hesitate to encumber their property with a permanent conservation easement for fear that the property's value will be diminished should they or their children wish to sell the ranch or use the property as collateral for a loan. But on the other hand, the conservation arrangement, by lowering the ranch's value (and thus inheritance taxes on it), can make it easier for ranchers to pass on their property to their children, a painfully expensive proposition under the current tax laws. Too often a large federal tax burden forces heirs to sell part or all of an operating ranch to pay the inheritance taxes, destroying both the integrity and the efficiency of the ranch in the process.

Harry McClure's ranch, for example, was sold a few years ago to pay the federal inheritance taxes. Ken Sodowsky, Harry's grandson and one of the heirs to his estate, told me recently about the sale: "Of course we wanted to keep ranching, but the taxes eat the place up. What did the government ever do to work the ranch, improve it, and make it productive? Nothing. By taking their tax bite, they took the ranch away from us. You bet I'm bitter about it." Most of the McClure Ranch was sold in one piece, but the man who bought it wasn't a rancher; he was the owner of a satellite television network from Denver.

It is ironic that urban money has preserved the rural countryside and its traditional way of life. Not too long ago, before the rural West became a haven (if not an escape) from the horrors of the American city, ranching provided the economic rationale for an open landscape. Now it is the urban resident—the dreaded city slicker—who can best afford to save and preserve the western countryside from the forces that have trashed the suburban landscape. One can only hope that if and when the present wealthy owners of Ouray County's showplace ranches decide to sell, their land will not be subdivided and the landscape of the county radically altered.

There are, of course, no guarantees that the county's open space will be preserved. If the bloom falls off the western rose and the region trashes itself in a frenzy of economic development (including tourism), the large landowners who sought refuge in the beauty of Ouray County and similar areas throughout the Rockies might just decide to sell out and seek their privacy elsewhere—the Sonoran Desert, perhaps, or in Argentina's Patagonia region. Of course, the best protection for the county's open ranchland would be a significant and permanent increase in the price of livestock. But county officials are as ineffective at influencing national cattle prices as they are at changing national tax policies.

But for all the good the new ranchers have done in protecting the open space of the county, their status as part-time summer residents isolates them from the community at large. Because they do not live in Ouray County year-round, they know little about the quality of the school, the infrastructure requirements of the county, or the general needs and aspirations of the county's full-time residents. Hidden and secure on their own land, the newcomers deliberately segregate themselves from their neighbors and the townspeople. Their wealth sets them apart from the full-time residents.

When the people of a community, large or small, share common external threats (such as a government agency or an unpopular law), they form a bond that encourages and sometimes forces cooperation. In the late nineteenth century, Ouray County residents were brought together by their shared dislike of the gold standard. In the 1930s, virtually all residents suffered from the economic woes brought on by the Depression. Today, a midwestern industrialist vacationing on his ranch in Ridgway may have to worry about a strike for higher wages at his manufacturing plant back home, but he neither knows nor cares when the Forest Service scales back his neighbor's, or even his own, summer grazing permit. He is financially immune to a three-month drought that devastates local hay production and forces smaller operators to sell off cattle at distressed prices. He complains loudly to the state Division of Wildlife that elk are feasting on his hay meadows and writes angry letters to the state saying that he should be compensated for the loss; but at the same time, he refuses to allow locals, including a needy neighbor, to hunt on his "private" property.

Summertime residents and locals may share a political party affiliation, but for entirely different reasons. The summer ranchers vote for politicians who will provide them with tax breaks, including corporate subsidies, and a friendly business environment for their respective businesses, be it oil and gas, manufacturing, or the medical and legal professions. They care little about health care for those who cannot afford it, adequate crop insurance, or increased retirement benefits, or such local issues as better roads, schools, and social services. Resident ranchers want the government, particularly the Forest Service, the EPA, and the Department of the Interior, to say out of their business.

＊

Ouray County today is not the place I moved to in 1974. Then, ranching and mining dominated the economy, and almost all of the county's income came from the ground. From the 1880s until the county's last large commercial mine (the Camp Bird) closed in the mid-1980s, there existed a reciprocity between agriculture and mining. Miners supplemented their incomes by working on hay crews in the summer, and some ranchers, when cattle prices weakened, worked in the mines in the winter. Today, more than half the income of Ouray County's residents is derived from dividends, interest, rent, and transfer payments. Retirees far outnumber ranchers and their employees. There are still more cattle than people, but the ratio is lessening. Land that twenty years ago went begging at two hundred dollars an acre now sells easily at eight to ten thousand dollars per acre. The agricultural extension service, once the handmaiden to the cattle industry, now receives more inquiries about dog and lawn care than it does about nutrition and inoculation requirements for livestock. And one is more likely to see spandexed bikers or sweating joggers on county roads than a herd of cattle or a band of sheep.

Nevertheless, there are places and people that haven't changed at all over the last quarter of a century. The post office is still the town's midmorning social center, although a letter addressed to a ranch that omits the box number or road address will no longer be delivered. Listeners to the Montrose radio station (KUBC) still receive daily corn, cattle, and hog prices right after the local hospital announcements (births, admissions, departures) and before the midday Paul Harvey news report. Ridgway's side streets remain unpaved. Henry and Mike Potter rise with the sun to irrigate their hay meadows with a shovel just as their father and three generations of valley ranchers have done for a century. Roger Noble, who followed his father as the county water commissioner, checks headgates throughout the county to ensure that no one takes more than his or her allotted share of the water. His good-natured counsel adds to the sense of neighborliness among ranchers, particularly in a dry year. Dave Wood, the president of the Citizens State Bank, will, if he knows you, make a character loan in defiance of modern loan practices. Randy Jones, the local state trooper, tickets speeding drivers with all the courtesy of a friendly uncle. Walt Orvis can dress out an elk with as much skill as any nineteenth-century trapper. And Mario Zadra, well into his eighties, can still, if he has to, put a rope on an ornery bull running full bore through a grove of aspens and snub it to a tree while he doctors it for foot rot. Like the other older ranchers, men and women, he carries forward the considerable skills of the cowboy-stockman.

Ridgway is a far more diverse and interesting place now than it was when I moved into Ouray County in 1974. The new medical center at the old site of the county maintenance shop has brought better and more convenient medical care to the entire area population. A roof truss factory stands today in the old rail yard and supplies its product to home builders throughout western Colorado; a tepee manufacturer fills orders from around the country; and the manufacturer of climbing skins for cross-county skiers ships its highly specialized product to Europe and Japan. A local craftsman manufactures the music industry's Grammy trophies, then sends them to Montrose to be gold-plated. A retail plant nursery now occupies the old school. The new shops and markets have brought a new economic vitality to the county. Where in the early 1980s Ouray County had one of the highest unemployment rates in the state—above 20 percent—today it is only slightly above the state's very low 4 percent average.

Resident artists and retired professionals lend their expertise to invigorated volunteer organizations such as EMTs, the Mountain Rescue Team, the Ouray County Historical Society, and the Performing Arts Guild. The True Grit Café and other restaurants provide healthy and tasteful alternatives to the Little Chef, where twenty years ago the Saturday night "road kill" special consisted of meat (species unknown) and potatoes (age unknown) glued together by an unrecognizable bonding agent. The live music and crowded dance floor at The Big Barn on Saturday nights are a vast improvement over the ten scratchy selections on the Little Chef's old jukebox. There's still no traffic light in the county, although there is more than enough traffic to justify one.

On Sunday afternoons in the mid-1970s, I'd join some friends at the Little Chef bar to drink a few beers and watch the Broncos game on the bar's TV, which got the best reception in town (but still plenty of snow). If the game was dull, we'd place bets on how many cars would pass the front window during the second half. The one who guessed less than five usually won. Today, a guess of seventy-five would lose you a cold Coors on the low side. Even though they're reluctant to admit it today, the old-timers agree that Ridgway is a more interesting place to live now.

————•·•·———

Like other rural Americans in the late twentieth century, Ridgway's residents are better connected to the larger world than we were a quarter of a century ago. I shared my first ranch telephone line with six other ranches, and only in a dire emergency would I dare to cut in and request a free line; today, I have two private lines, and with my fax and modem I can pull up timely stock market reports (both livestock and corporate) not only from Chicago and New York but also from Tokyo and London. One friend, a former Wyoming rancher, told me not long ago why he quit the cattle business: "With the assistance of my computer, I made more money in one day on a hi-tech stock trade than I did all year with my hay-eating, four-legged critters. And it didn't take me too damned long to figure out which stock market was going to pay my daughter's college tuition."

The social fabric of the place has altered as well. Ridgway's population is still all white and predominantly Protestant, but it lacks the relative economic equality that characterized the first- and second-generation residents. In the old days, the few "poor" residents were cared for by the county and the community at large.

The two largest landowners, Marie Scott and Harry McClure, were as much a part of the community as the cowboys who worked for them or the electricians who came out from town to rewire their barns. Marie supported everything from the Volunteer Fire Department to the local cemetery board. She looked after her employees, like Jim Harrison, who in good times and bad had given her the hard work and devoted service she expected. Harry McClure served for years as a county commissioner and was so well respected that anyone who didn't get along with him wouldn't dare admit it, or so his grandson Ken Sodowky says. Harry's Thursday night poker game included large landowners as well as wage workers. He helped his neighbors during roundups and brandings and never turned down a legitimate request for assistance (including loans) from his friends, of whom he had many. Owners of vast acreage, Harry and Marie considered themselves land rich but cash poor.

The old-time ranchers' fear that they are in danger of being replaced by a new landed gentry is accompanied by a dread that the gentrification process will transform Ridgway into another Telluride or Aspen, where the tourist industry has created a "servant economy." Telluride's development followed a distinctive pattern. First, it was "discovered" as one of the last "unspoiled" towns in the Rockies. Entrepreneurs and real estate developers came and built luxury lodges, trophy homes, expensive restaurants, and the other amenities demanded by the rich and famous. Hollywood stars moved in, and they attracted corporate moguls and the idle rich. Range Rovers came to outnumber pickups. And the old-timers, who couldn't afford the higher taxes required to pay for the new services demanded by the newcomers, moved out.

There is no business in Telluride today that can replace a car transmission, unplug a sewer line, or sell household appliances. The folks who can afford to live there and who run the place—its schools, government, and services—are mostly trust-fund recreationists who, with their year-round leisured lifestyles, have transformed a working-class community into an expensive playground. Authorities in Aspen and Telluride have tried to attract and hold a working class by offering housing subsidies, but their efforts have failed. Only in Aspen would "workers" with incomes up to $120,000 a year qualify for "affordable housing."

Fortunately, Ridgway and Ouray County—unlike Vail, Jackson Hole, and Aspen—have retained a large middle class of shopkeepers, retirees, artists, skilled craftsmen, and wage earners who have not yet been displaced by the escalating land values, although the process has started. How to keep the full-time residents whose skills are needed in the area is a major concern of old-timers and newcomers alike. Dave Calhoun, a former county commissioner, asserted for years in public meetings the need to keep the "lunch pail set" in the county, recognizing that all residents need auto mechanics, carpenters, and plumbers. A new county commissioner, Frank Hodsoll, a high-ranking White House official in the Reagan and Bush administrations and now a full-time Ridgway resident, emphasized the importance of maintaining the county's economic diversity in his successful bid to become one of the few county commissioners born outside the county.

On the other hand, people who move to the area with too much debt and too few skills discover early that the western dream does not live for them in Ridgway. As their resources shrink and the dream withers, some depart (mostly back to California); others hang on to a marginal existence in trailer parks, rented cabins, or shacks that barely meet minimum housing standards. The county sheriff's office and social services department blame this group of residents for the increased number of domestic violence cases, almost three times the number a decade ago, with battered women and abused and orphaned children the most common incidents.

———·•·———

Although the physical and demographic changes in Ridgway and the surrounding countryside are clearly evident, the changes in human relationships are less perceptible, if no less significant. Residents are less intimate with each other than they were in the mid-1970s. It wasn't all that long ago that residents traded their labor with each other out of personal friendship and a shared sense of community responsibility. No one kept an accounting of how much labor was given and how much was received because no one was willing to equate or reduce personal relationships to a definite value; not because it couldn't be done by some sophisticated mental calculus, but because it was inappropriate, even rude, to even attempt such a calculation. Everyone knew that labor and assistance were mutually shared, in good times and bad.

Cash was a rare commodity when most of the county's older

residents were growing up. In its place, ranchers and townsfolk used barter to obtain what they needed. A couple of tons of fresh grass hay might entice a neighbor to part with a healthy yearling heifer. A young horse not yet fully trained might fetch a used saddle needing only slight repair. Slowly, however, as cash became the predominant transactional mechanism, bartering disappeared and the habit of neighboring weakened. Once ranchers had come to depend on a national market that demanded cash for all purchased goods and services, the habit and necessity for barter transactions, even at the local level, diminished.

At the same time, cash attained the power to disintegrate personal relationships and weaken the social fabric of places such as Ridgway. People with a lot of cash do not have to depend on barter, traditional support networks, and local institutions. Don Caddy, a lifelong resident and recently retired county commissioner, observed: "The dollar is the big thing now. Before, it was neighbor helping neighbor."

There used to be a friendliness, even with strangers, that is lacking today. People waved as they passed you in a vehicle. The greeting, no doubt a habit carried over from horse-and-carriage days when travelers were happy to see another human on a trail or backcountry road, was a courtesy extended to everyone on the road. The greeting took on the form of an informal salute, given off the right eyebrow with the right index finger. There were even regional differences in the greeting. Rural visitors from northern Colorado moved the left hand from right to left in a slow wave. Those passing through from the eastern plains offered a casual wave of the left hand, only barely visible above the dashboard. Not many people wave anymore in Ouray County. I don't know why we've lost this cultural signal, but it probably has as much to do with the constant stream of traffic (we'd never stop waving) as it does with the anonymity brought on by the sudden growth of the county's population.

It is the old-timers who feel most severely the loss of their familiar world and its attendant value system. They see themselves as outsiders in an urban culture that views rural symbols and values as old-fashioned, like a set of worn-out, out-of-style clothes. They remember a time when anyone with a good herd of cattle on a medium-sized ranch could get ahead in the world. The fortunes of ranchers and townspeople alike rose or fell on the price of cattle. They celebrated their triumphs and suffered their losses together. And they recognized that when wealth came to a neighbor, it derived from hard work performed right there in the county, not outside it.

The Old West doesn't have much regard for the New West. When local ranchers look at a hobby ranch with its fancy equipment and cattle, all purchased with money earned elsewhere, they are reminded that it is now impossible for their sons and daughters to buy a place of their own. There is a feeling, at least in Ridgway, that if the "instant" ranchers had not come, the older generation of stockmen could have preserved their businesses and lifestyle. Old-timers tend to view the county's new absentee landed gentry as the modern-day equivalent of the lords and earls John Kettle wanted to distance himself from when he departed Victorian England in the mid-nineteenth century. What are the consequences for a place when nonresidents own most of the land? Absentee ownership does not enhance the mechanics of democracy Thomas Jefferson had in mind when he purchased the West from the French.

What I personally find most troubling about the new ranchers is not the way they gained their wealth, or their radically different lifestyles, but the historical disconnection between them and the county's older residents. The newer residents have little knowledge or appreciation of the history that produced the skills and survival trails carried forward by three generations of local citizens. If they even think of the homesteaders' experience, it is in terms of *Little House on the Prairie*. Hollywood has so warped the homestead experience, wrapping it in a nostalgic cocoon, that newcomers cannot recognize or accept a past that runs counter to the celluloid creation. As for the Depression, it is best forgotten because it is so depressing. The new owner of a Colorado, Wyoming, or Montana ranch does not wish to be confronted with evidence that might challenge, if not negate, his or her romanticized version of western history. Colorado historian Patricia Limerick is no doubt correct when she says that "people with money get to determine whose fantasy rules."

———•◦•———

The old-timers will tell you that cows and people don't mix. People want enclosures while cattle seek open space, and the best cattle country is that with the fewest people. Ed and Linda Ingo, third-generation ranchers whose family ranch on the edge of Ridgway is now nearly surrounded by houses and subdivisions, would agree. Like other area ranchers, they are obliged to spend more and more of their time defending in public hearings and court their historic agricultural water and property rights against people who have no appreciation or knowledge of agriculture. Domestic water wells and a nearby gravel operation have dried up a critical spring. Fences built decades ago when land values were a tenth of their current value must be moved to the surveyed boundaries. Linda Ingo recently observed: "God said 'love thy neighbor.' But I ask, why so many?"

A few local environmentalists have suggested that there are too many cattle and not enough wolves, bears, coyotes, and prairie dogs in the vicinity, particularly on public lands. They also think wolves and grizzly bears should be reintroduced into the area, an idea that has met with almost unanimous opposition locally. The ranchers view environmentalists, especially the "boutique preservationists," as an annoying pack of affluent eastern tree huggers who would, in their ignorance of the West and their own hypocrisy, lock up valuable rangeland into summer playgrounds for recreationists and so limit cattle grazing as to endanger the livestock industry and the local businesses that depend on it. Why is it, some of my rancher friends ask, that environmentalists are the first to foul their own nests back home while always wanting to "save the West" for themselves?" "You should mind your own business," one rancher said at a recent Forest Service meeting in Delta, Colorado. "We don't stick our noses into the ways ... you foul the Hudson River or lay waste to a West Virginia coal valley. Maybe we should introduce wolves and grizzlies in Central Park."

Finally, there are some residents, old-timers mostly, who fear that the area is being transformed into a leisure colony. That in the process of trying to attract tourists, we, the residents of Ridgway, have become the stereotypical Westerners tourists seek (and pay to see) in the fantasy West. For all the money tourism generates, it is not a benign economic activity. Most local residents do not want to be maids, chair-lift operators, and waitresses serving the growing tourist trade. Is not Trail Town, for example, a creation designed specifically to conform to what tourists want to believe about Ridgway and the West? Have we not, in submitting to this nostalgic dynamic, allowed commercial hucksters to write our history and tell our story? In the process, have we not lost both our identity and our soul?

Visitors to the baggage claim area in the Montrose airport today are confronted by a large lighted advertisement, a massive display of three color photographs advertising a new housing development on what was until recently a huge sheep ranch overlooking Telluride. The largest color photograph is of the San Juan Mountains with a full moon rising in a purple sky over the snow-capped peaks. Another photo shows aspen groves within the development, which, the ad tells readers, offers "generous homesites, breathtaking views ... and all the conveniences of contemporary living." The third photo is of a grizzled old man wearing a cowboy hat and a well-trimmed white beard, looking out wistfully from a window framed in weathered barn wood.

The advertisement is an exercise in pure nostalgia. Its message is, "Buy a piece of a sheep ranch and relive the simple, healthy life amid the quaking aspens of the San Juans." The ad says nothing, of course, about the recent demise of the sheep industry in the United States, or that natural predators and foreign competition have destroyed the business.

I knew the old man in the picture. Charlie Cristelli was a retired sheepherder who came to this country as a seven-year-old in 1920, an impoverished Italian boy from Toronto whose father had been killed in the Great War. Charlie worked as a herder for several sheep outfits in southwestern Colorado and performed odd jobs at various local mines and on Marie Scott's ranch. I first encountered him in 1974 on my ranch when, just before the deer season opened, I noticed someone with a rifle crawling through a patch of willows along the irrigation ditch behind the house. I went out to investigate and found Charlie. I asked him what he was doing hunting out of season and on our ranch without permission, and he responded immediately, "No comprende inglés." I responded, not knowing Charlie to be Italian-born but fluent in English: "Aquí, no bang bang, comprende?" "Sí, senor," Charlie said in his best Spanish accent. He stood up, emptied the chamber of his old .30 caliber Winchester, and headed toward the road.

Later I came to know Charlie under different circumstances. When not herding for the Aldasoro sheep outfit above Telluride, he made his home in a camp trailer just up the road from our ranch on Marie Scott's old place. I'd see him from time to time during the summer, and always on Labor Day weekend in Ridgway wherever Slim and his sidekick from Telluride set up their gambling parlor. Charlie loved to gamble, and he'd spend almost the entire weekend at Slim's tables playing blackjack or shooting craps. In the winter, he'd take whatever savings survived Labor Day to the tables in Vegas. Charlie was best known for his trapping (coyote and bear) skills, particularly his recipe for coyote bait—a mixture of rotten trout mixed in a jar with coyote urine that was pure ambrosia to the killers stalking the lambs under Charlie's care.

By any measure, Charlie lived a hard life, too often consuming too much booze and tobacco and sometimes finding too little shelter and not enough food. He died of cirrhosis of the liver, penniless, in 1996. Charlie's photo may sell real estate, but his life is no model for the American Dream.

Chapter Eight

Conclusion

Our first autumn in Ridgway, the Potter family asked Deedee and me to help them move their herd of Hereford cows and calves from their ranch south of Ridgway to our ranch on Dallas Creek where the cows would winter. We had gotten to know Jack Potter and his family over the summer. Henry and Mike, Jack's two sons, had given me useful lessons in the intricacies of flood irrigation, and Jack himself, a slight, wiry man with cold blue eyes set in a handsome face cracked by hard work, offered me good advice on what kind of cattle did best in the mountains. Always wearing his black Stetson and a pair of high-topped boots with old-fashioned underslung riding heels, Jack could recount Hereford breeding lines back into the nineteenth century, a time when he would have felt very comfortable. Most people said Jack still carried the bark on his exterior, but in fact his rather sullen countenance hid a shy but thoughtful and dedicated cattleman. If you hung around Jack, you learned the business the hard, old-fashioned way—not by talk but by work.

The cattle drive would be relatively easy, Jack said. We'd trail the cattle down the county road off his ranch north into Ridgway and then move them around the edge of town to the base of the hill. Here we'd rest the cattle and let them cool off, and have a sandwich and some coffee ourselves before making the final four-mile climb up the hill on the state highway and on over to our ranch. It was a cool November day, but the midday sun was warm, and I shed my jacket just before we stopped for lunch on the western edge of town. After a very short break at the bottom of the hill, Jack said we needed to get moving. The wind was starting to blow hard out of the west, and like all experienced stockmen, he could smell a storm long before it arrived. We mounted and started moving the cattle up the Ridgway hill. When we were about halfway to the top, it started to snow. The accompanying wind bit at our faces, blowing straight at us and the cattle, who wanted nothing to do with the storm and made unsuccessful sorties to break away and return to the protection of Ridgway. We had just about topped the hill, pushing and even whipping on some of the recalcitrant stragglers, when a semi came over the lip too fast, hit its air brakes, and let out a high, loud screech. That was the final reason the cows needed to break ranks. They scattered like a covey of quail. Some turned straight back on Henry and Jack, and the others flew off to their north flank and down a steep embankment, with Mike, Deedee, and me helpless to stop them. One minute we had 150 cattle moving in a controlled drive, the next there were isolated pockets of cattle all through the town: in the school-yard, in front of the Little Chef saloon, and wandering through Ridgway's side streets. I saw Isabel McDonald, an older lady who once ran a boardinghouse for railroad workers, swatting at the bovine invaders with a house broom while trying unsuccessfully to scare three others out of what remained of her sizable summer garden.

After reconnoitering the situation with obvious disgust, Jack rounded up some not entirely sober reinforcements from the Little Chef to help us reassemble the herd. By late afternoon, we had the cows and calves gathered and tried once again to conquer Ridgway hill. We topped the hill as it turned dark, and with the aid of car headlights we pushed and shouted the cold, tired cattle through the storm the rest of the way to our ranch. The next week, the town passed an ordinance forbidding cattle drives through town.

That cold November night I counted only three house lights on the four-mile journey from the western edge of Ridgway to the ranch on Dallas Creek. Today, with new subdivisions covering the surrounding hillsides and houses encroaching in the valley, I can count almost fifty. The highway that was once an infrequently used path out to the few ranches on Dallas Creek and Pleasant Valley is now crowded with traffic headed to and from Telluride. Today, there's no need for an ordinance forbidding cattle drives in Ridgway; no rancher would think of putting his herd at risk before the constant onslaught of Porsches and pickups. Where, I ask myself, will the growth end? Will ranching survive? Should it survive?

Assuming Americans' continued desire for beef, there is no reason to believe cattle ranching is endangered in the United States. But the outlook for ranchers who must compete for land in a recreational/ tourist economy is not bright. Everyone wants the ranches to survive, if only to keep the landscape attractive and green and to maintain the open spaces. But high-priced land and profitable cattle operations are not compatible. Selling off land to compensate for low cattle prices is counterproductive, and buying land to expand the operation is financially impossible. Zoning will save some open space, and conservation easements will also help, but they are not for everyone, particularly those who require additional income to survive.

We may be able to save our farms and ranches, and the people who work them, with government subsidies of crop and livestock prices. But for every positive effect of a subsidy, there always seems to be an unintended negative consequence; it is as difficult as it is politically disturbing to investigate, much less understand, the layered complexity of these direct and indirect, state and federal, subsidies. Although they complain about them, it is questionable whether American taxpayers would really wish to do away with agricultural and energy subsidies, which guarantee to us an inexpensive and almost inexhaustible food supply.

What seems unfair is that the people who produce our food—who sustain our lives—can be so easily displaced from their land. Even when the sale is voluntary, the cash received never seems to be an adequate or even an appropriate replacement for the land—its grass and streams, its soils, its memories, and particularly its permanence. Like the Utes before them, almost all of Ridgway's pioneer families have now been separated from their land; the former were pushed by the military, but both were bought off with cash. The recycling of people on and off the land will continue as in the past, through time and space. Only the timing of the cycles appears to fluctuate.

As the area's working ranches have disappeared, so too have the skills and work habits that the land forced on (and into) the old-time ranchers. No matter how cranky and ornery they were (and are), the old-timers—people like Marie Scott, Harry McClure, and Jack Potter—wore the mark of the place and its weather, and possessed a hard-earned authenticity that seems lacking in the people who have replaced them. The newer folks don't possess the same survival skills, and they don't carry the history of the place they want to call home; nor do most of them, in their nostalgic dream world, even care to learn it. The character of Ridgway has changed. The play ethic is not the same as the work ethic.

Ridgway, in its new and physical and demographic diversity, is today less comfortable with itself, more suspiciously guarded in its human relations, and more isolated into separate groups. We don't know each other as well as we did when the county had fewer people and we were intimately connected through work and play. Too many flimflam men have come through town with false promises—like the folks from the Bureau of Reclamation who in the 1960s promised nirvana with the flooding of the town, or the new real estate agents who sell dreamscapes to willing buyers. Growth is not a win-win game for everyone. There have been winners, yes, but there have been losers too, and the losers continue to see growth as a zero-sum tragedy.

Yet for all the reserve that guards us from one another, there is also a greater tolerance for ideas and opinions not commonly held.

Virtually everyone now recognizes that the change that has hit Ridgway, at an uncomfortable velocity for some, can be controlled and intelligently planned for by local citizens without the "assistance" of intrusive advisers or outside experts. There is also within the county a courage and a proactive vision that seeks to ensure that whatever change does occur benefits the vast majority of residents. In this sense, Ridgway remains, for all the remnants of its historical provincialism, a pleasant place to live, work, and raise a family. It is why the Ingo family stays in Ridgway, why my family maintains a home here, and why other ranching families recognize that Ridgway has more to offer off the ranch than ever before.

The larger question facing Ridgway, and the other small rural towns that are becoming attractive places to live as technology frees an increasing number of citizens from the confines of urban living, is how to absorb the new residents who seek community in a small-town atmosphere. We like to look back into our history and recognize the times and circumstances when a sense of community was strong, when people came together to share not only common experiences but also common goals. And it is to small towns like Ridgway and Ouray that we look back with a certain longing, if not nostalgia, and say: "Look at the wonderful world we have lost. How do we recapture it?"

I am not at all certain that most citizens, if offered a clear and uncluttered view of the past, would really wish to recapture it, or at least all of it. Not many people today would choose the hardships of frontier life in western Colorado over the comforts of modern life. Nor would they care to live amidst the intolerance of the 1920s or relive the years of the Depression, which started early in the 1920s here and continued into the 1940s. What we long for is not the simple, hard life but the sense of community that has existed in Ridgway and other small towns from time to time.

Ethnic and religious differences aside, people back then did cooperate with each other. People worked at maintaining a sense of community and recognized its importance because it gave emotional and economic support in time of need. They shared common experiences, bartered among themselves for goods and services, and intermarried. They worked and played together as much out of necessity as out of choice. And even in the good times of the 1950s and 1960s, residents felt a pride in and attachment to Ridgway, which through its church, school, and community events and organizations cemented people to the place.

The earlier community fell apart not because residents let it happen but because so many of those who carried the memory and talent to create, sustain, and maintain a community died or moved away. The community literally could not sustain or re-create itself. The world around Ridgway changed. Local shops couldn't compete with the larger stores, and their cheaper prices, in Montrose. Television intruded into family time and community events. Small mountain ranch operations that survived, and at times prospered, with 150 cows could not compete in an industry in which profitability required a minimum of 300 cows. Nor did it help the community that the mines closed because of stricter environmental laws and foreign competition. Certainly the national government did the community no favor when it threatened to flood their town.

As it rebuilds itself today, Ridgway, with its influx of new residents, is also re-creating a community, not one modeled on or suitable for the late nineteenth century, but one appropriate for the twenty-first century. Through an historical lens clouded by nostalgia, we like to look back on earlier times and envision small towns and villages as warm and fuzzy places. But in its earlier days, the Ridgway community had its drawbacks. Because so many values were shared and so little debate that might challenge or question those values was tolerated, internal dissension rarely upset the serenity of the town. In many of the small western farm and ranch communities like Ridgway (and no doubt in other regions of the country) where democracy was supposed to have flourished, it actually stagnated in an atmosphere of quiet resignation, if not intolerance. For a century, Ridgway was an insular, one-dimensional, and proudly isolated place. Rarely challenged, either from the outside or from within, its internal value system served well most of its citizens. Residents rarely debated the established norms; they either accepted them, remained quiet, or moved to a more comfortable environment.

Ridgway today is not a community in the traditional sense. It is a much noisier and more contentious place than it was before, and, ironically, a more homogeneous one in terms of language, ethnic background, and even religion. The issues that divide the citizenry—growth, the school curriculum, zoning, affordable housing—cause constant, some say interminable, discussion and debate. But the debates that sometimes engulf the town and seem to citizens so destructive to a "sense of community" have, in fact, reinvigorated a democratic spirit. If a community is a place where people struggle in a climate of noisy but tolerant discourse toward a set of shared goals, then Ridgway is today a far stronger, more vibrant and democratic, and certainly far more interesting place than ever before in its relatively short history. It used to be said of Ridgway that the people were as cold as the winter weather and as hard and unforgiving as the mountainous terrain. Not so today.

Maybe Emerson was correct when he said that Americans "must regard the land as a commanding and increasing power on the citizen, ... which promises to disclose new virtues for ages to come." At a time when so much of our larger national culture, particularly our schools, is encouraging us to become specialists, so that we may quarrel with each other more effectively from our isolated cells, it is heartening to know that new, stronger communities can grow and flourish.

Ridgway may be losing its cows, but in the process it is gaining in human strength to sustain and comfort its citizens.

Courtesy of Hilary Decker

Peter R. Decker has had a varied career—merchant seaman, army officer, war correspondent for the Associate Press in Vietnam and Laos, college professor, rancher, and government official. After receiving his Ph.D. from Columbia University, he taught American history at Barnard College and Columbia, and public policy and history at Duke University. Since his permanent move to Colorado in 1980, Decker has served on Colorado's Commission on Higher Education, as commissioner of agriculture under Governor Roy Romer, and as a director of the Center of the American West.

Currently Decker is a director of the National Western Stock Show, and he continues to operate his cattle ranch in Ridgway, Colorado. He is the author of various articles and two other books, *Fortunes and Failures*, a study of San Francisco's nineteenth-century merchants, and *"The Utes Must Go!"*, the story of the expulsion of the majority of Colorado's first residents from the state.

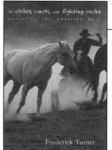